P9-DMW-249

THE BERKELEY SERIES IN AMERICAN HISTORY

# Adams and Jefferson: "Posterity Must Judge"

Edited by

## ADRIENNE KOCH

UNIVERSITY OF CALIFORNIA AT BERKELEY

RAND McNALLY & COMPANY · CHICAGO

*The Berkeley Series in American History*
*Charles Sellers, editor*

# CONTENTS

# INTRODUCTION

OF ALL PERIODS IN AMERICAN HISTORY, THE MOST CREATIVE IN POLITICAL thought and in the invention of political instrumentalities was the half century from 1765–1815. For in this period a full-bodied theory of constitutional government and a range of principles and procedures were developed that set us firmly on the path of representative democracy in America. The period spanned the developing arguments for separation from Great Britain culminating in the Declaration of Independence, the efforts to establish securely a new nation culminating in the Constitution, and the first critical steps in realizing republican government under a two-party system. Each of these three major phases presented wholly new problems and illustrated a revolutionary development maturing, unlike other revolutionary movements, into durable and representative political institutions continuous with the initial revolutionary spirit. Action, thought, debate, and conflict were called for on local, state, and ultimately continental levels and required internal measures and external policies embracing both war and peace.

A host of men contributed to one or another phase of this revolutionary and constructive political history, but some were men of heroic mold whose labors and creativity left their mark on the entire period. Foremost among the titans were George Washington, Benjamin Franklin, John Adams, Thomas Jefferson, James Madison, and Alexander Hamilton. Of these, Adams and Jefferson influenced the entire period and were equal to the many diverse and complex challenges initiated during this unprecedented "age of experiments." More than any others they trained themselves, by study and by political experience, to serve as the most profound philosopher-statesmen of republican government in America. Jefferson and Adams were, indeed, *the pair* of contemporaries whose moral, intellectual, and political traits were more evenly matched than were any other leaders of the day; and they were also the pair who had enough in common and enough at variance to exemplify the meaning of the American experiment to create and sustain a free government under law.

It is unnecessary to emphasize Jefferson's profound influence over his American fellow-citizens from his day to our own. For there is some truth in the view that, in the words of Henry Steele Commager, "Jefferson is the central figure in American history and—if freedom and democracy survive in our generation—he may yet prove to be the central figure in modern history." The influence of John Adams, on the other hand, has been lamentably slight—almost nonexistent as an explicit awareness on the part of the American people of their debt to him and their inheritance from him. Of this fate, Adams was himself the gloomy prophet. "Mausoleums, Statues, Monuments will never be erected to me . . . Panegyrical Romances will never be written, nor flattering orations spoken to transmit me to Posterity in brilliant colors." (To Benjamin Rush, March 23, 1809.) Nevertheless, the students of John Adams and his works have begun to see in the depth of his humanistic scholarship and intellectual curiosity that he was on a lofty eminence which only Jefferson could match. This truth Vernon Parrington, the liberal "Jeffersonian" historian, perceived and perhaps over-stated when he wrote that Adams "in spite of his dogmatisms and inconsistencies . . . remains the most notable political thinker . . . among American statesmen." In recent years, the advocates of "New Conservatism" (Russell Kirk, Peter Viereck, Clinton Rossiter) have claimed John Adams as their progenitor, as the American counterpart of Edmund Burke.

Both Thomas Jefferson and John Adams were complex men and minds who cannot be reduced to slogans nor captured for temporary movements. Timeless moral and political insights elevate their writings to the most creative level of political reflection. As men who led the colonies to independence and helped to keep an independent nation free, their characters and careers—in and out of office—are limitlessly absorbing to study. We will undertake our brief encounter with them aided by their own writings and, as much as possible, by their correspondence with each other. The reader's ultimate judgment may turn out to coincide with the conventional one that the difference between Adams and Jefferson is that between "conservative" and "liberal"; but even in that event, it should be a richer understanding and a more grounded knowledge than these elastic and sometimes fraudulent terms convey by themselves.

In the encounter with the thought of Adams and Jefferson, many questions press for an answer. Were the differences between these two great philosopher-statesmen substantial differences about the ends or only the methods of government? Were they more purely temperamental differences, sectional differences, class differences, or so tangled a skein of accidental and environmental influences (on each man) that *nothing* meaningful on the level of political thought and moral principle can be said about them?

It is well known that Jefferson and Adams, who esteemed and valued each other so highly, rather painfully edged into the role of political enemies in an estrangement that first manifested itself publicly in 1791, only to harden into a full-fledged break in friendship in the troubled atmosphere of the Alien and Sedition Acts in 1798. The olive branch was not heartfully tendered by either man until the first day of the year 1812; but by then Jefferson and Adams were living in retirement. They were wiser, mellower and thus better able to exemplify that Golden Rule which they both constantly invoked as their highest ideal. This dramatic pattern of friendship, estrangement, and reunion raises questions of interpretation:

I. Were the differences that were expressed as divergent political allegiances in New York, Philadelphia, and Washington in the decade of the 1790's and the first decade of the nineteenth century of earlier origin?

II. Were there any fundamental differences between them on the level of political thought and commitment when they were both ardent leaders in the Revolutionary movement, both early believers in natural law and natural rights, both advocates of a "manly" American independence and Republican government, both lawyers versed in the common law tradition of England and in Parliamentary history as well as in the international law of the great seventeenth-century Continental jurists?

III. Were temperamental *and* theoretical differences in belief present but not acute in the years when Jefferson and his daughters and John and Abigail Adams and their children were intimate friends as they carried on their diplomatic missions in France, Holland, and England?

IV. On the other hand, did they begin with a common position only to develop differences after the American Republic was on its own, as a new nation, and they became vice presidents and presidents? Was "politics" rather than "principle" the cause of their later differences?

V. Or, finally, shall we invade the dim world of the cradle and place a two-dimensional prefabricated "personality type" graph on it, emphasizing John Adams' own comment (very late in life) that when he visited a foundling nursery in Paris he could detect at once the "inequalities" between the various infants, some being nervous, weak, sickly; others strong, contented, placid, or bold? Jefferson who liked, as he said, "to grasp things by the smooth handle" was in this regard unlike his friend who seemed by nature prone perpetually to grasp a porcupine's quills.

These questions could be elaborated, and they could all be made much more detailed. Yet even as they now appear, it should be evident that there will be no easy, and perhaps no definitive, answers. We are summoned to make a try, however, by the taunting echo of John Adams' pointed words to Jefferson: "Whether you or I were right Posterity must judge. . . ."

*I*

# INTELLECTUAL LEADERSHIP
# FOR INDEPENDENCE

To be sure, the early careers of Adams and Jefferson are comparable in many points. They were both ardent students, learned and philosophical in their approach to questions. They were united in a common love of books, and they read habitually at a pace and with a philosophic method that would be hard to match in our own, or in any, day. They both became successful lawyers in their respective colonies of Massachusetts and Virginia in very short order. And they both were drawn to an early entrance on the political scene and on the side of opposition to British Parliamentary rule by an eloquent defense of the liberties of British Americans.

### A.

### ADAMS' BACKGROUND

⁋Adams, as a person, and Massachusetts, as a colony, had a different character and history to bring to the uphill struggle for political rights than Jefferson and Virginia. Eight years older than Jefferson, he began to practice law in 1758 when Jefferson, a lad in his teens, was studying Greek and Latin. He was a self-conscious, self-scrutinizing, troubled and ambitious young man, very sensible of the fact that he was the first in his family to have had the opportunity to attend Harvard College and that it was his imperative duty to achieve something worthy in public life. In his Diary he argued with himself about the respective values of amassing a fortune or serving the community, and, while prominence and self-satisfaction were elements of both, the conflict was decided in favor of public service because of the moral sanction of reforming and improving the world about him. Since he was thrown by his college contacts and by his profession into a circle of "gentlemen" whose property and funds always outdistanced his own, he began early a life-long struggle to combine support for his family and financial respectability with the demanding tasks of his career.

[ 4 ]

Adams' career opened with his protest against the Stamp Act of 1765 when he identified himself as a spokesman for "the liberty side" against "the prerogative side" in Massachusetts. It was then that he wrote his first influential essays, "A Dissertation of Canon and Feudal Law" and the "Braintree Instructions." The "Dissertation" developed the theme that it was a struggle against *civil* as well as religious tyranny that peopled America: "It was not religion alone, as is commonly supposed; but it was a love of universal liberty, and a hatred, a dread, a horror, of the infernal confederacy [of the canon and feudal law] . . . that . . . accomplished the settlement of America." The "Instructions" denounced the Stamp Act as contrary to the English constitution and "directly repugnant to the Great Charter itself" because it involved taxation without representation and permitted judges to sit alone without juries to decide both the law and the facts.

In April 1768, Adams moved to Boston and solidified his leadership of the Whig forces by writing the "Boston Instructions." These protested the seizure of Hancock's sloop *Liberty* and the stationing of British troops to enforce the Townshend Acts. Inevitably, these Acts only exaggerated Adams' natural tendencies to try himself by soul-shaking tests. Soon after his protest, Jonathan Sewell visited him, acting as an emissary from Governor Bernard, to tempt the able young lawyer with the office of King's Advocate—an offer intended to wean him from his friends in the resistance and to tie him to the Crown. In the moment of choice Adams had to face the prospect that he might sacrifice immediate success, eventual wealth, and perhaps a splendid sphere of influence for a dubious and possibly ruinous cause and that the means for existence of his family (he had an infant son and a small girl at the time) were at stake. Adams made his hard choice almost instantly, the very evening he was tendered the offer.

It was his genius for "difficult cases" that led Adams to accept the defense of Captain Preston, the officer who had commanded the British soldiers in the "Boston Massacre" of 1770. Adams willingly braved the fury of his own political associates for this service to his cherished ideal of equal protection under law. Using a sentence which he quoted from the great Italian jurist Beccaria, he stated with considerable effect in opening the trial: "If, by supporting the rights of mankind, and of invincible truth, I shall contribute to save from the agonies of death one unfortunate victim of tyranny, or of ignorance equally fatal, his blessing and tears of transport will be a sufficient consolation to me for the contempt of all mankind."

### B.

## JEFFERSON'S BACKGROUND

❡In Jefferson, one senses a different personality and the different climate of history and customs in Virginia. He was a youthful participant in the social set of good Virginia families in his school and college days (at William and Mary), fond of bilingual puns and exaggerated phrases of rapture over the pretty young girls of his circle. In these younger days he also delighted in long canoe trips on the James River, was a fine horseman, an alert and advanced planter, and a man who knew how to build a house. But these activities did not reduce the brilliance of his mind, the habits of close study, or the range of his interests. A commonplace book of his readings in law and legal and political history provides a good notion of how careful a reader he was; another in which he entered literary excerpts from Greek and Roman philosophers, moralists, and poets strengthens the impression that he was seeking to clarify his moral philosophy at the same time that he found enchantment in the classical imagination and in its poetic forms. Somehow, Jefferson found time for loafing with friends and tempting his soul, while he placed orders for new books for his library with an insatiable appetite that only grew with the years. How much of this air of sunny good humor and pleasant living was a function of Jefferson's temperament? How much was part and parcel of the upper-class Virginia to which he belonged?

The comparative mildness of the struggle in Virginia in the years from 1763–1774 compared with the trials experienced in Massachusetts should not be misconstrued, however. For, despite the more secure and less intense manner of the Virginia planters who led the opposition forces, a certain boldness of both style and logic enabled them, in several instances, to proceed in advance of the Massachusetts leaders in the guidance of the continent. For example, patriot leaders like Patrick Henry, Richard Henry Lee, and Jefferson himself, acting as a standing committee of the Virginia House of Burgesses, were responsible for the first effective call in 1773 for an inter-colonial linkage of committees of correspondence. The correspondence committees which Sam Adams had taken the lead in setting up the year before had been primarily concerned with the towns throughout Massachusetts, and thus were provincewide rather than intercolonial. Even earlier, one might point to Virginia's leadership in speaking out against the Stamp Act. Again, although the call for the Stamp Act Congress issued from the Massachusetts Assembly, the Virginia Resolves which had been introduced in the House of Burgesses by Patrick Henry's "treason" speech had been enacted first and had been widely reported in colonial newspapers. Jefferson, almost from the time he was admitted to the bar and certainly from the opening of his public life, belonged to the group of bold, young patriot leaders like Patrick Henry and Richard Henry Lee, rather than to the more conservative ruling group of elder statesmen like John Robinson, Peyton Randolph, and Edmund Pendleton.

## C.

## YOUNG STATESMEN

⟨Both Adams and Jefferson were thus prepared to meet the new turn of events which the Boston Tea Party, on the night of December 26, 1773, signalized. The year 1774 was full of the consequences of what Abigail Adams called "that bainfull weed," the "weed of slavery." That year an angry Parliament passed the Coercive Acts which, as a first measure, closed the port of Boston. In response to this, the colonies made common cause with Massachusetts and the first Continental Congress met in Philadelphia. "There is a new and grand scene open before me, a Congress," Adams wrote in his Diary. "This will be an assembly of the wisest men upon the continent, who are Americans in principle." Unquestionably this was the year when "Americans in principle" would probe the fundamental questions of America's relationships with the British Empire in an effort to find formulas and formulations that would secure their liberties. Two of the most important formulations were provided by Jefferson in his *Summary View of the Rights of British America* and Adams in his "Novanglus" essays.

Jefferson's *Summary View* was written in August 1774, to guide the Virginia delegates to the First Continental Congress in preparing an address to the King protesting the coercive legislation of Parliament. Jefferson's paper was considered too bold at the time for acceptance by the Virginia delegates because it suggested good-bye to compromise. Nevertheless, it was printed and won fame quickly for Jefferson. In the view of Adams and others, Jefferson's reputation based upon this "handsome public paper" earned him the opportunity to draft the Declaration of Independence.

Adams' "Novanglus" essays appeared in the Boston *Gazette* in January 1775 and subsequently in weekly installments until April 19 when the battle of Lexington, as he wrote, "changed the instruments of warfare from the Penn to the Sword." These essays took the form of "letters" to the inhabitants of the Colony of Massachusetts Bay in answer to a series of "Tory" newspaper articles signed "Massachusettensis." Adams felt that the articles could not go unanswered by the Whig forces because "they were well written, abounded with Wit, discovered good Information, and were conducted with a Subtlety of Art and Address, wonderfully calculated to keep Up the Spirit of their Party, to depress ours, to spread intimidation and to make Proselytes." Adams, in no mood to keep silent with the timorous, took up the challenge.

Both of these writings defined the moral and political principles which animated the resistance in the American colonies just before independence was declared. They rehearsed the historical grievances, explored the nature of the British Empire, cited legal precedents, Parliamentary statutes, royal proclamations, and argued from the traditions of natural law and contract theory. Although there was a latent threat of taking action for full independence, the overt argument in each work attempted to establish American liberty *within* a framework of loyalty to the King.

In comparing these two works, it is important to determine where they agreed and where they differed. On the critical issue of Parliamentary right to legislate for the American colonies, what limits did each author stipulate? What were the limits to the right of revolution? What was the logic of obligation to the King? What did Adams mean when he appealed to "right reason"? And what did Jefferson mean when he appealed to "natural rights"? What elements of British tradition did each writer invoke in support of his position? Which argument, on the whole, was more cogent in logic and which one more cogent on the basis of the evidence adduced? Finally, can you detect any differences in scope and tone in view of the fact that Jefferson's piece was drafted for the Continental Congress by a Virginian and Adams' letters were addressed to the people of Massachusetts to controvert a Tory antagonist? (Adrienne Koch and William Peden eds., *The Life and Selected Writings of Thomas Jefferson* [New York: Random House, Inc., 1944], pp. 293–311; and Charles Francis Adams, ed., *The Works of John Adams*, 10 vols. [Boston: Charles Little and James Brown, 1851], IV, 11–177.)]

## *"A Summary View of the Rights of British America"*

RESOLVED, THAT it be an instruction to the said deputies, when assembled in General Congress, with the deputies from the other states of British America, to propose to the said Congress, that an humble and dutiful address be presented to his Majesty, begging leave to lay before him, as Chief Magistrate of the British empire, the united complaints of his Majesty's subjects in America; complaints which are excited by many unwarrantable encroachments and usurpations, attempted to be made by the legislature of one part of the empire, upon the rights which God, and the laws, have given equally and independently to all. . . .

To remind him that our ancestors, before their emigration to America, were the free inhabitants of the British dominions in Europe, and possessed a right, which nature has given to all men, of departing from the country in which chance, not choice, has placed them, of going in quest of new habitations, and of there establishing new societies, under such laws and regulations as, to them, shall seem most likely to promote public happiness. That their Saxon ancestors had, under this universal law, in like manner, left their native wilds and woods in the North of Europe, had possessed themselves of the Island of Britain, then less charged with inhabitants, and had established there that system of laws which has so long been the glory and protection of that country. Nor was ever any claim of superiority or dependence asserted over them, by that mother country from which they had migrated: and were such a claim made, it is believed his Majesty's subjects in Great Britain have too firm a feeling of the rights derived to them from their ancestors, to bow down the sovereignty of their state before such visionary pretensions. And it is thought that no circumstance has occurred to distinguish, materially, the British from the Saxon emigration. America was conquered, and her settlements made and firmly established, at the expense of individuals, and not of the British public. Their own blood was spilt in acquiring lands for their settlement, their own fortunes expended in making that settlement effectual. For themselves they fought, for themselves they conquered, and for themselves alone they have right to hold. . . .

That the exercise of a free trade with all parts of the world, possessed by the American colonists, as of natural right, and which no law of their own had taken away or abridged, was next the object of unjust encroachment. . . . History has informed us, that bodies of men as well as of individuals, are susceptible of the spirit of tyranny. A view of these acts of Parliament for regulation, as it has been affectedly called, of the American trade, if all other evidences were removed out of the case, would undeniably evince the truth of this observation. . . . But, that we do not point out to his Majesty the injustice of these acts, with intent to rest on that principle the cause of their nullity; but to show that experience confirms the propriety of those political principles, which exempt us from the jurisdiction of the British Parliament. The true ground on which we declare these acts void, is, that the British Parliament has no right to exercise authority over us. . . .

Not only the principles of common sense, but the common feelings of human nature must be surrendered up, before his Majesty's subjects here, can be persuaded to believe, that they hold their political existence at the will of a British Parliament. Shall these governments be dissolved, their property annihilated, and their people reduced to a state of nature, at the imperious breath of a body of men whom they never saw, in whom they never confided, and over whom they have no powers of punishment or removal, let their crimes against the American public be ever so great? Can any one reason be assigned, why one hundred and sixty thousand electors in the island of Great Britain, should give law to four millions in the States of America, every individual of whom is equal to every individual of them in virtue, in understanding, and in bodily strength? Were this to be admitted, instead of being a free people, as we have hitherto supposed, and mean to continue ourselves, we should suddenly be found the slaves, not of one, but of one hundred and sixty thousand tyrants; distinguished, too, from all others, by this singular circumstance, that they are removed from the reach of fear, the only restraining motive which may hold the hand of a tyrant. . . .

That we next proceed to consider the conduct of his Majesty, as holding the Executive powers of the laws of these States, and mark out his deviations from the line of duty. By the Constitution of Great Britain, as well as of the several American States, his Majesty possesses the power of refusing to pass into a law, any bill which has already passed the other two branches of the legislature. . . . Yet this will not excuse the wanton exercise of this power, which we have seen his Majesty practice on the laws of the American legislature. For the most trifling reasons, and sometimes for no conceivable reason at all, his Majesty has rejected laws of the most salutary tendency. The abolition of domestic slavery is the great object of desire in those colonies, where it was, unhappily, introduced in their infant state. But previous to the enfranchisement of the slaves we have, it is necessary to exclude all further importations from Africa. Yet our repeated attempts to effect this, by prohibitions, and by imposing duties which might amount to a prohibition, having been hitherto defeated by his Majesty's negative: thus preferring the immediate advantages of a few British corsairs, to the lasting interests of the American States, and to the rights of human nature, deeply wounded by this infamous practice. Nay, the single interposition of an interested individual against a law was scarcely ever known to fail of success, though, in the opposite scale, were placed the interests of a whole country. That this is so shameful an abuse of a power, trusted with his Majesty for other purposes, as if, not reformed, would call for some legal restrictions. . . .

That these are our grievances, which we have thus laid before his Majesty, with that freedom of language and sentiment which becomes a free people claiming their rights as derived from the laws of nature, and not as the gift of their Chief Magistrate. Let those flatter, who fear: it is not an American art. To give praise where it is not due might be well from the venal, but would ill beseem those who are asserting the rights of human nature. They know, and will, therefore, say, that Kings are the servants, not the proprietors of the people. . . . This, Sire, is the advice of your great American council, on the observance of which may perhaps depend your felicity and future fame, and the preservation of that harmony which alone can continue, both to Great Britain and America, the reciprocal advantages of their connection. It is neither our wish nor our interest to separate from her. We are willing, on our part, to sacrifice everything which reason can ask, to the restoration of that tranquillity for which all must wish. On their part, let them be ready to establish union on a generous plan. Let them name their terms, but let them be just. Accept of every commercial preference it is in our power to give, for such things as we can raise for their use, or they make for ours. But let them not think to exclude us from going to other markets to dispose of those commodities which they cannot use, nor to supply those wants which they cannot supply. Still less, let it be proposed, that our properties, within our own territories, shall be taxed or regulated by any power on earth, but our own. The God who gave us life, gave us liberty at the same time: the hand of force may destroy, but cannot disjoin them. This, Sire, is our last, our determined resolution. And that you will be pleased to interpose, with that efficacy which your earnest endeavors may insure, to procure redress of these our great grievances, to quiet the minds of your subjects in British America against any apprehensions of future encroachment, to establish fraternal love and harmony through the whole empire, and that that may continue to the latest ages of time, is the frevent prayer of all British America.

## "Novanglus"

Massachusettensis, conscious that the people of this continent have the utmost abhorrence of treason and rebellion, labors to avail himself of the magic in these words. But his artifice is vain. The people are not to be intimidated by hard words from a necessary defence of their liberties. Their attachment to their constitution, so dearly purchased by their own and their ancestors' blood and treasure; their aversion to the late innovations; their horror of arbitrary power and the Romish religion, are much deeper rooted than their dread of rude sounds and unmannerly language. They do not want "the advice of an honest lawyer, if such an one could be found," nor will they be deceived by a dishonest one. They know what offence it is to assemble armed, and forcibly obstruct the course of justice. They have been many years considering and inquiring; they have been instructed by Massachusettensis and his friends, in the nature of treason, and the consequences of their own principles and actions. They know upon what hinge the whole dispute turns; that the *fundamentals* of the government over them are disputed; that the minister pretends, and had the influence to obtain the voice of the last parliament in his favor, that parliament is the only supreme, sovereign, absolute, and uncontrollable legislative over all the colonies; that, therefore, the minister and all his advocates will call resistance to acts of parliament by the names of treason and rebellion. But, at the same time, they know that, in their own opinions, and in the opinions of all the colonies, parliament has no authority over them, excepting to regulate their trade, and this not by any principle of common law, but merely by the consent of the colonies, founded on the obvious necessity of a case which was never in contemplation of that law, nor provided for by it. . . .

The terms "British Empire" are not the language of the common law, but the language of newspapers and political pamphlets; that the dominions of the king of Great Britain have no power coextensive with them. I would ask, by what law the parliament has authority over America? By the law of God, in the Old and New Testament, it has none; by the law of nature and nations, it has none; by the common law of England, it has none, for the common law and the authority of parliament founded on it, never extended beyond the four seas; by statute law it has none, for no statute was made before the settlement of the colonies for this purpose; and the declaratory act, made in 1766, was made without our consent, by a parliament which had no authority beyond the four seas. What religious, moral, or political obligations then are we under to submit to parliament as a supreme legislative? None at all. When it is said, that if we are not subject to the supreme authority of parliament, Great Britain will make us so, all other laws and obligations are given up, and recourse is had to the *ratio ultima* of Louis XIV. And the *suprema lex* of the king of Sardinia,—to the law of brickbats and cannon balls, which can be answered only by brickbats and balls. . . .

Such events as the resistance to the Stamp Act, and to the Tea Act, particularly the destruction of that which was sent by the ministry, in the name of the East India Company, have ever been cautiously spoken of by the whigs, because they knew the delicacy of the subject, and they lived in continual hopes of a speedy restoration of liberty and peace. But we are now thrown into a situation, which would render any further delicacy upon this point criminal.

Be it remembered, then, that there are tumults, seditions, popular commotions, insurrections, and civil wars, upon just occasions as well as unjust.

Grotius B. 1, c. 3, § 1, observes, "that some sort of private war may be lawfully waged. It is not repugnant to the law of nature, for any one to repel injuries by force". . . . [Adams here cites at length from Grotius, Sidney and Locke to develop the theme that "the general insurrection of a whole nation does not deserve the name of a rebellion."]

If there is any thing in these quotations, which is applicable to the destruction of the tea, or any other branch of our subject, it is not my fault; I did not make it. Surely Grotius, Pufendorf, Barbeyrac, Locke, Sidney, and Le Clerc, are writers of sufficient weight to put in the scale against the mercenary scribblers in New York and Boston, who have the unexampled impudence and folly, to call these, which are revolution principles, in question, and to ground their arguments upon passive obedience as a corner stone . . . we must go to the bottom of this great controversy. If parliament has a right to tax us, and legislate for us in all cases, the destruction of the tea was unjustifiable; but if the people of America are right in their principle, that parliament has no such right, that the act of parliament is null and void, and it is lawful to oppose and resist it, the question then is, whether the destruction was necessary; for every principle of reason, justice, and prudence, in such cases, demands that the least mischief shall be done, the least evil, among a number, shall always be preferred. . . . All men will agree that such steps ought not to be taken but in cases of absolute necessity, and that such necessity must be very clear. But most people in America now think the destruction of the Boston tea was absolutely necessary, and therefore right and just. . . .

That "the colonies owe no allegiance to any imperial crown," provided such a crown involves in it a house of lords and a house of commons, is certain. Indeed, we owe no allegiance to any crown at all. We owe allegiance to the person of his majesty, King George III., whom God preserve. But allegiance is due universally, both from Britons and Americans to the person of the king, not to his crown; to his natural, not his politic capacity. . . .

Thus, we see, that in every instance which can be found, the observation proves to be true, that, by the common law, the laws of England, the authority of parliament, and the limits of the realm, were confined within seas. That the kings of England had frequently foreign dominions, some by conquest, some by marriage, and some by descent. But, in all those cases, the kings were either absolute in those dominions, or bound to govern them according to their own respective laws, and by their own legislative and executive councils. That the laws of England did not extend there, and the English parliament pretended no jurisdiction there, nor claimed any right to control the king in his government of those dominions. And, from this extensive survey of all the foregoing cases, there results a confirmation of what has been so often said, that there is no provision in the common law, in English precedents, in the English government or constitution, made for the case of the colonies. It is not a conquered, but a discovered country. It came not by marriage to the king, but was purchased by the settlers of the savages. It was not granted by the king of his grace, but was dearly, very dearly earned by the planters, in the labor, blood, and treasure which they expended to subdue it to cultivation. It stands upon no grounds, then, of law or policy, but what are found in the law of nature, and their express contracts in their charters, and their implied contracts in the commissions to governors and terms of settlement.

# CONSTITUTIONS AND
# INDEPENDENCE: 1776

ADAMS SAID THAT THE BATTLE OF LEXINGTON CHANGED THE INSTRUMENTS of warfare from the pen to the sword. Yet even in the midst of war, the sword had not really displaced the pen. Actually, in 1776, the pen—and the voice—were mightier than ever. Both of these powers were used for debating, planning, resolution drafting, pamphleteering, and modeling new state governments, as well as in behalf of an immortal manifesto. Jefferson, who some years later had occasion to prepare notes for his *Summary View*, commented that "my creed was formed on the unsheathing of the sword at Lexington."

## A.

### STATE CONSTITUTION-MAKERS

❡One of the most important activities that engaged Adams and Jefferson was that of giving thought to the kind of government that should replace the colonial one in order to secure the rights of Americans against tyranny. Adams noted that "almost every day I had something to say about Advizing the States to institute Governments." He viewed this as the "real engine of independence." For he saw independence itself as "Sampson, pulling down, unless the people also— preferably first—build up the house in which they will live." On May 10, 1776, Congress adopted his resolution recommending that the colonies assume all the powers of government. On May 15, the Virginia Convention acted on this recommendation, adopted its famous resolution calling for independence, and appointed a committee to draft a new plan of state government. Jefferson, who had arrived in Philadelphia to join Congress the day before, wrote Thomas Nelson suggesting that he be recalled with other delegates to Virginia to help in the drafting of the new state constitution. "In truth it is the whole object of the present controversy; for should a bad government be instituted for us in future it had been as well to have accepted at first the bad one offered to us from beyond the water without the risk and expence of contest."

Adams and Jefferson themselves made two of the most substantial contributions toward the creation of state government in this period. Adams wrote the "Thoughts on Government." He prepared this extraordinary document in the form of a "letter" to George Wythe of Virginia some time before April 20, 1776. Jefferson wrote three different drafts of the proposed constitution for Virginia before June 13, 1776. (The selection printed below is from the third draft.) Although Jefferson had to remain in Philadelphia, he sent on his draft of the constitution to Virginia. It arrived too late for full consideration, but it did influence the final document adopted by the Convention in several important ways: the entire preamble was adopted and in several instances Jefferson's ideas and very language were employed.

In reading these two documents we should ask: What did Adams and Jefferson consider basic criteria for "republican" government? What assumptions about human nature and history were reflected in their proposals? What provisions were made for suffrage and representation in each contsitution? What safeguards were provided in each model for individual liberties? for social reforms? What type, if any, amending procedure did each constitution stipulate? Finally, what differences do you see in the nature of executive power? (Adrienne Koch and William Peden, eds., *Selected Writings of John and John Quincy Adams* [New York: Knopf, 1946], pp. 51–57 and Julian P. Boyd and others, eds., *The Papers of Thomas Jefferson* [Princeton: Princeton Univ. Press, 1950—], I, 356-64.)]

*"Thoughts on Government"*

MY DEAR Sir: If I was equal to the task of forming a plan for the government of a colony, I should be flattered with your request and very happy to comply with it because, as the divine science of politics is the science of social happiness, and the blessings of society depend entirely on the constitutions of government, which are generally institutions that last for many generations, there can be no employment more agreeable to a benevolent mind than a research after the best. . . .

We ought to consider what is the end of government before we determine which is the best form. Upon this point all speculative politicians will agree that the happiness of society is the end of government, as all divines and moral philosophers will agree that the happiness of the individual is the end of man. From this principle it will follow that the form of government which communicates ease, comfort, security, or, in one word, happiness to the greatest number of persons and in the greatest degree is the best. . . .

Fear is the foundation of most governments; but it is so sordid and brutal a passion and renders men in whose breasts it predominates so stupid and miserable that Americans will not be likely to approve of any political institution which is founded on it. . . .

A man must be indifferent to the sneers of modern Englishmen to mention in their company the names of Sidney, Harrington, Locke, Milton, Nedham, Neville, Burnet, and Hoadly. No small fortitude is necessary to confess that one has read them. The wretched condition of this country, however, for ten or fifteen years past has frequently reminded me of their principles and reasonings. They will convince any candid mind that there is no good government but what is republican. That the only valuable part of the British constitution is so because the very definition of a republic is "an empire of laws, and not of men.". . .

As good government is an empire of laws, how shall your laws be made? In a large society inhabiting an extensive country, it is impossible that the whole should assemble to make laws. The first necessary step, then, is to depute power from the many to a few of the most wise and good. But by what rules shall you choose your representatives? Agree upon the number and qualifications of persons who shall have the benefit of choosing or annex this privilege to the inhabitants of a certain extent of ground.

The principal difficulty lies, and the greatest care should be employed, in constituting this representative assembly. It should be in miniature an exact portrait of the people at large. It should think, feel, reason, and act like them. That it may be the interest of this assembly to do strict justice at all times, it should be an equal representation, or, in other words, equal interests among the people should have equal interests in it. Great care should be taken to effect this and to prevent unfair, partial, and corrupt elections. . . .

A representation of the people in one assembly being obtained, a question arises whether all the powers of government—legislative, executive, and judicial—shall be left in this body? I think a people cannot be long free, nor ever happy, whose government is in one assembly. My reasons for this opinion are as follow:

1. A single assembly is liable to all the vices, follies, and frailties of an individual. . . .

2. A single assembly is apt to be avaricious. . . .

3. A single assembly is apt to grow ambitious and after a time will not hesitate to vote itself perpetual. . . .

4. A representative assembly . . . is unfit to exercise the executive power for want of two essential properties, secrecy and dispatch.

5. A representative assembly is still less qualified for the judicial power because it is too numerous, too slow, and too little skilled in the laws.

6. Because a single assembly, possessed of all the powers of government, would make arbitrary laws for their own interest, execute all laws arbitrarily for their own interest, and adjudge all controversies in their own favor.

But shall the whole power of legislation rest in one assembly? Most of the foregoing reasons apply equally to prove that the legislative power ought to be more complex, to which we may add that if the legislative power is wholly in one assembly and the executive in another or in a single person, these two powers will oppose and encroach upon each other until the contest shall end in war, and the whole power, legislative and executive, be usurped by the strongest. . . .

To avoid these dangers, let a distinct assembly be constituted as a mediator between the two. . . .

Let the representative assembly then elect by ballot, from among themselves or their constituents or both, a distinct assembly which, for the sake of perspicuity, we will call a council. . . .

These two bodies, thus constituted and made integral parts of the legislature, let them unite and by joint ballot choose a governor, who . . . should have a free and independent exercise of his judgment. . . . As the governor is to be invested with the executive power with consent of council, I think he ought to have a negative upon the legislative. . . .

In the present exigency of American affairs, when by an act of Parliament we are put out of the royal protection and consequently discharged from our allegiance, and it has become necessary to assume government for our immediate security, the governor . . . should be chosen by joint ballot of both houses. And these and all other elections, especially of representatives and counsellors, should be annual, there not being in the whole circle of the sciences a maxim more infallible than this, "where annual elections end, there slavery begins.". . .

The dignity and stability of government in all its branches, the morals of the people, and every blessing of society depend so much upon an upright and skillful administration of justice that the judicial power ought to be distinct from both the legislative and executive, and independent upon both, that so it may be a check upon both, as both should be checks upon that. . . .

Laws for the liberal education of youth, especially of the lower class of people, are so extremely wise and useful that to a humane and generous mind no expense for this purpose would be thought extravagant. . . .

A constitution founded on these principles introduces knowledge among the people and inspires them with a conscious dignity becoming freemen. . . .

You and I, my dear friend, have been sent into life at a time when the greatest lawgivers of antiquity would have wished to live. How few of the human race have ever enjoyed an opportunity of making an election of government—more than of air, soil, or climate—for themselves or their children! When, before the present epocha, had three millions of people full power and a fair opportunity to form and establish the wisest and happiest government that human wisdom can contrive? I hope you will avail yourself and your country of that extensive learning and indefatigable industry which you possess to assist her in the formation of the happiest governments and the best character of a great people. . . .

## Jefferson's Draft Constitution for Virginia

[Third Draft, before 13 June 1776]

A bill for new-modeling the form of Government and for establishing the fundamental principles thereof in future.

Whereas George Guelf, king of Great Britain and Ireland and Elector of Hanover, heretofore entrusted with the exercise of the kingly office in this government, has endeavored to pervert the same into a detestable and insupportable tyranny by putting his negative on laws the most wholesome and necessary for ye public good. . . .
[Here follows a list of a long "train of abuses," like those in *A Summary View* and later in the *Declaration*.]

Be it therefore enacted by the authority of the people that the said George Guelf be, and he hereby is, deposed from the kingly office within this government and absolutely divested of all its rights, powers and prerogatives . . . . and that the said office shall henceforth cease and never more either in name or substance be re-established within this colony.

And be it further enacted by the authority aforesaid that the following fundamental laws and principles of government shall henceforth be established:

The Legislative, Executive, and Judiciary offices shall be kept forever separate and no person exercising the one shall be capable of appointment to the others, or to either of them.

### I. Legislative

Legislation shall be exercised by two separate houses, to wit, a house of Representatives and a house of Senators, which shall be called the General Assembly of Virginia.

The said house of Representatives shall be composed of persons chosen by the people annually. . . .

All male persons of full age and sane mind having a freehold estate in one fourth of an acre of land in any town or in 25 acres of land in the country, and all persons resident in the colony who shall have paid scot and lot to government the last two years shall have right to give their vote in the election of their respective representatives. . . .

### II. Executive

The executive powers shall be exercised in manner following:

One person to be called the Administrator shall be annually appointed by the house of Representatives on the second day of their first session, who after having acted one year shall be incapable of being again appointed to that office until he shall have been out of the same three years. . . .

The Administrator shall possess the powers formerly held by the king, save only that:

he shall be bound by acts of legislature though not expressly named;

he shall have no negative on the bills of the legislature. . . .

### III. Judiciary

[There follows a description of the judicial system, providing among other things for trial by jury and establishing a system of county courts.]

## IV. Rights Private and Public

Every person of full age neither owning nor having owned fifty acres of land shall be entitled to an appropriation of fifty acres or to so much as shall make up what he owns or has owned fifty acres in full and absolute dominion, and no other person shall be capable of taking an appropriation. . . .

No person hereafter coming into this country shall be held within the same in slavery under any pretext whatever. . . .

All persons shall have full and free liberty of religious opinion; nor shall any be compelled to frequent or maintain any religious institution. . . .

Printing presses shall be free, except so far as by commission of private injury cause may be given of private action. . . .

None of these fundamental laws and principles of government shall be repealed or altered, but by the personal consent of the people on summons to meet in their respective counties on one and the same day by an act of Legislature to be passed for every special occasion; and if in such county meetings the people of two thirds of the counties shall give their suffrage for any particular alteration or repeal referred to them by the said act, the same shall be accordingly repealed or altered, and such repeal or alteration shall take its place among these fundamentals and stand on the same footing with them, in lieu of the article repealed or altered. . . .

### B.

# POSTSCRIPT ON THE DECLARATION OF INDEPENDENCE

❧In "The Thoughts on Government" and the "Draft Constitution For Virginia," we can see an agreement on the fundamentals of liberty which made it possible for Adams and Jefferson to join forces in the committee of the second Continental Congress to draft a Declaration of Independence. No one knew that this particular committee assignment would have more to do with immortality than with treason, punishment, or annihilation.

Jefferson was asked to submit a draft because, as Adams wrote in his *Autobiography*, "Mr. Jefferson had the reputation of a masterly pen; he had been chosen a delegate in Virginia, in consequence of a very handsome public paper which he had written for the House of Burgesses, which had given him the character of a fine writer." When Jefferson submitted his draft only a few, minor verbal changes were made.

But Adams again played an invaluable role, defending the Declaration when it came up for consideration on the floor of Congress. Jefferson testified to the supreme service Adams rendered in securing the vote for the Declaration of Independence. "He was the pillar of its support on the floor of Congress, its ablest advocate and defender against the multifarious assaults it encountered." Where Jefferson used his pen, Adams used his voice to become (in Jefferson's words) *"the* Colussus" of Independence.]

*III*

# THE VAUNTED SCENE OF EUROPE: 1780's

## *A.*

### FRIENDSHIP ABROAD

In the spring of 1784, when Adams was already a veteran overseas diplomat of some six years standing, Jefferson was appointed to join Franklin and him in negotiating treaties of commerce. Jefferson arrived in Paris in August 1784, at about the same time that Abigail Adams, with her daughter, Abigail, came to join her husband. Adams had written a relative that he was awaiting Jefferson's arrival as "an old Friend . . . with whom I have often had occasion to labour at many a knotty Problem." What actually developed, despite marked temperamental differences between the two men, was an affectionate friendship. In January 1787, Jefferson had occasion to write confidential estimates of the "public characters" he was working with to Madison, who had for some years been a harsh critic of Adams' faults. Jefferson's estimate of Adams, however, was discriminating and hardheaded, but undeniably affectionate. (Boyd, *Jefferson Papers*, XI, 94–95.)]

You know the opinion I formerly entertained of my friend Mr. Adams. Yourself and the governor were the first who shook that opinion. I afterwards saw proofs which convicted him of a degree of vanity, and of a blindness to it, of which no germ had appeared in Congress. A 7-months' intimacy with him here and as many weeks in London have given me opportunities of studying him closely. He is vain, irritable and a bad calculator of the force and probable effect of the motives which govern men. He is as disinterested as the being which made him; he is profound in his views: and accurate in his judgment except where knowledge of the world is necessary to form a judgment. He is so amiable, that I pronounce you will love him if ever you become acquainted with him. He would be, as he was, a great man in Congress.

[While the two men were working together in Paris, Jefferson spent many pleasant hours at the Adams' residence. He soon became a good friend of Abigail Adams, too, for she was spirited, upright, witty, and intellectual. John Quincy Adams, then a young man in his late teens about to return to Cambridge to study at Harvard, was also a favorite of Jefferson's. When Jefferson succeeded to Franklin's place as minister plenipotentiary to France and Adams, in May 1785, had to begin his residence in London as the first American minister to the court of St. James, Adams was, he confessed, "triste" at parting with his friend. Jefferson, in a return letter was more explicit: "The departure of your family has left me in the dumps. My afternoons hang heavily on me." When Jefferson learned that Adams would return to the United States in June 1788, there was no trace of insincerity in his declaration to his older friend that he was "overwhelmed" to learn the news. (Boyd, *Jefferson Papers*, XI, 170.)]

I LEARN with real pain the resolution you have taken of quitting Europe. Your presence on this side of the Atlantic gave me a confidence that if any difficulties should arise within my department, I should always have one to advise with on whose counsels I could rely. I shall now feel bewidowed.

[The tone of this letter speaks for itself. Jefferson's usual restraint is gone. He even invents a word, "bewidowed" (somewhat like his more famous Americanism: "belittle"), to give force to his sense of deprivation.

## B.

## DISAGREEMENT ABOUT SHAYS' REBELLION

⟨Bearing in mind the predominantly smooth course of Jefferson's and Adams' relationship in their joint years of diplomatic service abroad, one might fail to do justice to the humor, the complications, and the tensions—some aired openly, some submerged out of the requirements of friendship—in their relationship. More important, however, than the injustice of homogenizing these two interesting human beings would be the consequent distortion of their political principles that would ensue. If one studies the full correspondence of each of these men during the most affectionate period of their association in France and London, especially in the years from 1786 through 1788, the evidences of incompatible and hard differences may already be detected, symbolized by their divergent reactions to Shays' Rebellion, the first serious outbreak in Massachusetts since the Revolution.

When the news of Shays' Rebellion first was carried to the American diplomats abroad, John Adams received it calmly enough, remarking to Jefferson in his first mention of it (November 30, 1786), "Don't be alarmed at the late Turbulance in New England. The Massachusetts Assembly had, in its Zeal to get the better of their Debt, lain on a Tax, rather heavier than the People could bear; but all will be well, and this Commotion will terminate in additional strength to Government." Reports on the continuing series of armed invasions of the courts by western Massachusetts farmers and former revolutionary officers and soldiers kept coming to Adams from correspondents like John Jay, Colonel Benjamin Hichborn, and Rufus King. These men were appalled at the "present convulsion in this State."

More significant still were the letters which Abigail Adams received from her two sisters, Mary Cranch and Elizabeth Shaw. Mary Cranch's letters were particularly bitter, since her husband, Judge Richard Cranch (Adams' best friend from college days as well as brother-in-law), had suffered financially from the insurgents' interference with the courts and the rebellion against the payment of taxes. Mrs. Cranch complained to her sister: "Mr. Cranch has been labouring for the Publick for three or four years without receiving scarcely any pay. . . . Mr. Cranch . . . says he must come home & go to watch mending & Farming & leave the public business to be transacted by those who can afford to work without pay. What will be the end of these things I am not Pollititien enough to say. They have a most gloomy appearance." (Braintree, September 24, 1786, Adams Manuscript Trust, microfilm reel 368.)

There is little doubt that Mrs. Adams discussed her deep concern with her husband and that the situation of his near-family registered painfully upon his judgment of the events. The "feebleness" of the Massachusetts government, its failure to afford security, or to assert its authority had dismayed friends whose political sagacity he valued—Jay, Hichborn, King, and others. What added flame to Adams' feelings was the inference that the Rebellion was partly directed against the Massachusetts Constitution which he had drafted and that one of the popular threats made by the insurgents was to get rid of the Senate and "reform" the government into a single house assembly.

Most startling is a letter he wrote to John Jay on the same day that he penned his "don't worry" comment to Jefferson. "The just complaints of the people of real grievances ought never to be discouraged and even their imaginary grievances may be treated with too great severity," he conceded. "But when a Cry is Set up for the abolition of Debts, equal Division of Property, and the abolition of Senators and Governors it is time for every Honest Man to consider his Situation. . . . The Laws alone Can secure any Man his own Body, Estate or Peace of Mind and if these are scorned in God's name what is ever to be respected. What is there worth living for?" (Grosvenor Square, November 30, 1786, Letterbook, Adams Manuscript Trust, microfilm reel 112.)

These views became more severe with the continuing series of rebellious acts in the cold winter of 1786–1787, and by January 27, 1787, he was confiding to Benjamin Hichborn his conviction that liberty could *never* comport with flaunting the law and mob violence. He asked: "Is not a Shattuck or a Shays as great a tyrant, when he would pluck up law and justice by the roots, as a Bernard or a Hutchinson, when he would overturn them partially?"

The divergence in outlook between Jefferson and Adams on the Rebellion in Massachusetts is revealed, interestingly, through Mrs. Adams' correspondence with the normally soft-spoken and considerate Virginian. Incensed by what she had heard from home and read in the Boston newspapers which were forwarded to her, Mrs. Adams undertook to report on "the tumults in my native state." (Boyd, *Jefferson Papers*, XI, 86.)]

IGNORANT, WRESTLESS desperadoes, without conscience or principals, have led a deluded multitude to follow their standard, under pretense of grievances which have no existence but in their imaginations. . . . By this . . . you will see the materials which compose this rebellion, and the necessity there is of the wisest and most vigorous measures to quell and suppress it. Instead of that laudible spirit which you approve, which makes a people watchfull over their Liberties and alert in the defence of them, these mobish insurgents are for sapping the foundation and distroying the whole fabrick at once.

[Jefferson replied to this letter some three weeks later, in a tone of asperity and even indignation, that had previously appeared nowhere in his correspondence with either of the Adamses. In fact, his own growing interest in the reform movement in France which would eventuate in the Revolution was uppermost in his thoughts in this period, as his reports to Adams, who could not have shared his sympathies, reveal. Moreover, Abigail Adams' harsh condemnation of the rebels and their supporters were not easy for him to tolerate. He wrote, therefore, an extreme statement of his own stand. (P. L. Ford, ed., *The Writings of Thomas Jefferson*, 10 vols. [New York: Putnam, 1893], IV, 369–70.)]

I AM to acknowledge the honor of your letter of Jan. 29. and of the papers you were so good as to send me. They were the latest I had seen or have yet seen. They left off too in a critical moment; just at the point where the Malcontents make their submission on condition of pardon, and before the answer of government was known. I hope they pardoned them. The spirit of resistance to government is so valuable on certain occasions, that I wish it to be always kept alive. It will often be exercised when wrong, but better so than not to be exercised at all. I like a little rebellion now and then. It is like a storm in the Atmosphere.

[In this conflict of opinions, do you see an irreconcilable conflict of political ends? or merely means? Is Adams repudiating or reaffirming the real principles of the American Revolution? Is the issue properly stated as a contrast between an essentially "conservative" revolution for independence versus a "liberal" continuing revolution for successive social reform? Or is the reason for the disagreement simply that Adams was judging on the basis of more detailed information about the economic and political situation in Massachusetts?

It is against this setting that one should view the political reflections on the fundamentals of free society in which Jefferson and Adams were engaged in the 1780's while they observed the contrasts between European monarchies and American constitutional forms of government. Each man published a book during his ambassadorship abroad in which their ideas reached definitive formulation.

Jefferson had completed his manuscript, *Notes on the State of Virginia*, while still at home. He took it with him to Paris, where it was first printed in 1785 in a small private edition. After several subsequent editions he authorized a trade edition in London in 1787. The book contained a wealth of information about the social conditions, manners, climate, flora and fauna, geography and culture of Virginia—all in a pattern of answers to queries from the French Minister in Philadelphia. Most important, it contained the celebrated "philosophical legislation of Virginia," which formulated, as Jefferson once said, "my general principles of government."

Jefferson's efforts to revise the Virginia code of laws in the three years succeeding Independence resulted in some 125 bills. Of all of them, Jefferson testified to his choice of the bill for religious freedom as the most important. He named this bill and the Declaration of Independence as the two political acts for which he wished to be remembered. The following excerpt is an explanation of the philosophy which led Jefferson to provide for the complete separation of church and state. (Koch and Peden, *Jefferson*, pp. 274–76.)]

## Notes on the State of Virginia

THE ERROR seems not sufficiently eradicated, that the operations of the mind, as well as the acts of the body, are subject to the coercion of the laws. But our rulers can have no authority over such natural rights, only as we have submitted to them. The rights of conscience we never submitted, we could not submit. We are answerable for them to our God. The legitimate powers of government extend to such acts only as are injurious to others. But it does me no injury for my neighbor to say there are twenty gods, or no God. It neither picks my pocket nor breaks my leg. If it be said, his testimony in a court of justice cannot be relied on, reject it then, and be the stigma on him. Constraint may make him worse by making him a hypocrite, but it will never make him a truer man. It may fix him obstinately in his errors, but will not cure them. Reason and free inquiry are the only effectual agents against error. Give a loose to them, they will support the true religion by bringing every false one to their tribunal, to the test of their investigation. They are the natural enemies of error, and of error only. . . . It is error alone which needs the support of government. Truth can stand by itself. Subject opinion to coercion: whom will you make your inquisitors? Fallible men; men governed by bad passions, by private as well as public reasons. And why subject it to coercion? To produce uniformity. But is uniformity of opinion desirable? No more than of face and stature. Introduce the bed of Procrustes then, and as there is danger that the large men may beat the small, make us all of a size, by lopping the former and stretching the latter. Difference of opinion is advantageous in religion. The several sects perform the office of a *censor morum* over each other. Is uniformity attainable? Millions of innocent men, women, and children, since the introduction of Christianity, have been burnt, tortured, fined, imprisoned; yet we have not advanced one inch towards uniformity. What has been the effect of coercion? To make one half the world fools, and the other half hypocrites. To support roguery and error all over the earth. Let us reflect that it is inhabited by a thousand millions of people. That these profess probably a thousand different systems of religion. That ours is but one of that thousand. That if there be but one right, and ours that one, we should wish to see the nine hundred and ninety-nine wandering sects gathered into the fold of truth. But against such a majority we cannot effect this by force. Reason and persuasion are the only practicable instruments. To make way for these, free inquiry must be indulged; and how can we wish others to indulge it while we refuse it ourselves.

[Another bill concerning the revisal of Virginia's laws to which Jefferson attached special importance was the bill "to diffuse knowledge more generally through the mass of the people." (Koch and Peden, *Jefferson*, pp. 263–65.)]

THE GENERAL objects of this law are to provide an education adapted to the years, to the capacity, and the condition of every one, and directed to their freedom and happiness. . . . By that part of our plan which prescribes the selection of the youths of genius from among the classes of the poor, we hope to avail the State of those talents which nature has sown as liberally among the poor as the rich, but which perish without use, if not sought for and cultivated. But of the views of this law none is more important, none more legitimate, than that of rendering the people the safe, as they are the ultimate, guardians of their own liberty. For this purpose the reading in the first stage, where *they* will receive their whole education, is proposed, as has been said, to be chiefly historical. History, by apprizing them of the past, will enable them to judge of the future; it will avail them of the experience of other times and other nations; it will qualify them as judges of the actions and designs of men; it will enable them to know ambition under every disguise it may assume; and knowing it, to defeat its views. In every government on earth is some trace of human weakness, some germ of corruption and degeneracy, which cunning will discover, and wickedness insensibly open, cultivate and improve. Every government degenerates when trusted to the rulers of the people alone. The people themselves therefore are its only safe depositories. And to render even them safe, their minds must be improved to a certain degree. This indeed is not all that is necessary, though it be essentially necessary. An amendment of our constitution must here come in aid of the public education. The influence over government must be shared among all the people. If every individual which composes their mass participates of the ultimate authority, the government will be safe.

[One of the most interesting replies in the *Notes* is devoted to the question of the Virginia Constitution of 1776. Jefferson's criticism of that instrument reveals some of his characteristic political beliefs in the 1780's. (Koch and Peden, *Jefferson*, p. 237.)]

ALL THE powers of government, legislative, executive, and judiciary, result to the legislative body. The concentrating these in the same hands is precisely the definition of despotic government. It will be no alleviation that these powers will be exercised by a plurality of hands, and not by a single one. One hundred and seventy-three despots would surely be as oppressive as one. Let those who doubt it turn their eyes on the republic of Venice. As little will it avail us that they are chosen by ourselves. An *elective despotism* was not the government we fought for, but one which should not only be founded on free principles, but in which the powers of government should be so divided and balanced among several bodies of magistracy, as that no one could transcend their legal limits, without being effectually checked and restrained by the others.

[About a year after the first publication of Jefferson's *Notes*, John Adams worked at top speed in London gathering notes and composing his massive three-volume treatise, *A Defence of the Constitutions of Government of the United States of America*. His first volume appeared in London in January 1787, the second followed in September, the third in 1788. In writing it, Adams had four motives: First, Shays Rebellion, the upheaval in his native state, induced him to try to instruct his countrymen about stable and balanced government in a critical era. Second, Adams was infuriated by the "pestilent county conventions" in Massachusetts and the political turmoil created by countless petitions and protests that, in his opinion, had not been backed by a decent knowledge of the rudiments of political science. Third, Adams sensed that a vast movement of social and political protest was gaining headway on the continent of Europe and that Europeans, as well as his fellow citizens at home, needed to know the results of an intensive search into the hearts of men, into their conduct as political beings, and into the historical lessons of the Western world on the prime subjects of constitutions and forms of government. Fourth, Adams was moved by a quasi-personal challenge. Turgot, the French philosopher and statesman, in 1778 had delivered an opinion, in a published letter to Dr. Richard Price, that the American state governments "instead of bringing all the authorities into one, that of the nation, they have established different bodies, a house of representatives, a council, a governor, because England has a house of commons, a house of lords, and a king." Adams wrote his three stout volumes to annihilate this four-page analysis of the thesis of "the nation in one center." (Koch and Peden, *Adams*, pp. 83–84.)]

## A Defence of the Constitutions of Government of the United States of America

THE PEOPLE in America have now the best opportunity and the greatest trust in their hands that Providence ever committeed to so small a number since the transgression of the first pair; if they betray their trust, their guilt will merit even greater punishment than other nations have suffered and the indignation of Heaven. If there is one certain truth to be collected from the history of all ages, it is this: that the people's rights and liberties and the democratical mixture in a constitution can never be preserved without a strong executive, or, in other words, without separating the executive from the legislative power. If the executive power or any considerable part of it is left in the hands either of an aristocratical or a democratical assembly, it will corrupt the legislature as necessarily as rust corrupts iron or as arsenic poisons the human body; and when the legislature is corrupted, the people are undone.

[Adams' reflections on the slippery term "equality" appear in the following selection from the *Defence*. How does he sustain his initial support of the revolutionary appeal to "equality" in the Declaration of Independence and his view that some men are more equal than others? What weight does he give to "moral and political equality" as against *actual* differences of inequality that appear within society, such as those associated with birth, wealth, ability, and chance? (Koch and Peden, *Adams*, pp. 95–96.)]

LET us now return to M. Turgot's idea of a government consisting in a single assembly. He tells us our republics are 'founded on the equality of all the citizens, and, therefore, "orders" and "equilibriums" are unnecessary and occasion disputes.' But what are we to understand here by equality? . . . Was there, or will there ever be, a nation whose individuals were all equal in natural and acquired qualities, in virtues, talents, and riches? The answer of all mankind must be in the negative. It must then be acknowledged that . . . . there are inequalities which God and nature have planted there, and which no human legislator ever can eradicate. . . .

In this society of Massachusettensians then there is, it is true, a moral and political equality of rights and duties among all the individuals and as yet no appearance of artificial inequalities of conditions . . . there are, nevertheless, inequalities of great moment in the consideration of a legislator, because they have a natural and inevitable influence in society. Let us enumerate some of them: 1. There is an inequality of wealth. . . . 2. Birth. Let no man be surprised that this species of inequality is introduced here. Let the page in history be quoted where any nation, ancient or modern, civilized or savage, is mentioned, among whom no difference was made between the citizens on account of their extraction. . . .

It will be readily admitted there are great inequalities of merit, or talents, virtues, services, and what is of more moment, very often of reputation. . . .

These sources of inequality, which are common to every people and can never be altered by any because they are founded in the constitution of nature—this natural aristocracy among mankind has been dilated on because it is a fact essential to be considered in the institution of a government. It forms a body of men which contains the greatest collection of virtues and abilities in a free government, is the brightest ornament and glory of the nation, and may always be made the greatest blessing of society if it be judiciously managed in the constitution. But if this be not done, it is always the most dangerous; nay, it may be added, it never fails to be the destruction of the commonwealth.

What shall be done to guard against it? . . .

There is but one expedient yet discovered to avail the society of all the benefits from this body of men which they are capable of affording, and at the same time to prevent them from undermining or invading the public liberty; and that is to throw them all, or at least the most remarkable of them, into one assembly together, in the legislature; to keep all the executive power entirely out of their hands as a body; to erect a first magistrate over them, invested with the whole executive authority; to make them dependent on that executive magistrate for all public executive employments; to give that first magistrate a negative on the legislature, by which he may defend both himself and the people from all their enterprises in the legislature; and to erect on the other side an impregnable barrier against them in a house of commons, fairly, fully, and adequately representing the people, who shall have the power both of negativing all their attempts at encroachment in the legislature and of withholding from them and from the crown all supplies by which they may be paid for their services in executive offices, or even the public service may be carried on to the detriment of the nation.

[On the basis of these arguments, Adams rebuts the maxims of radical (i.e. democratic) republican theory. (C. F. Adams, *Works*, VI, 65.)]

It is agreed that 'the end of all government is the good and ease of the people in a secure enjoyment of their rights without oppression'; but it must be remembered that the rich are *people* as well as the poor; that they have rights as well as others; that they have as clear and as *sacred* a right to their large property as others have to theirs which is smaller; that oppression to them is as possible and as wicked as to others; that stealing, robbing, cheating are the same crimes and sins, whether committed against them or others. The rich, therefore, ought to have an effectual barrier in the constitution against being robbed, plundered, and murdered, as well as the poor; and this can never be without an independent senate. The poor should have a bulwark against the same dangers and oppressions; and this can never be without a house of representatives of the people. But neither the rich nor the poor can be defended by their respective guardians in the constitution without an executive power, vested with a negative equal to either, to hold the balance even between them and decide when they cannot agree. . . .

## C.

## DIFFERENCES ON THE CONSTITUTION

❡This period of the friendship between Adams and Jefferson in Europe comes to a close with an exchange of their first impressions on the new federal constitution. It would have been extraordinary had they not found something to cavil at in that instrument—if for no other reason than that they each considered the work of creating new governments through the process of deliberate plan the most "splendid" and momentous occupation in which a man could engage. Yet it had been the lot of these two philosophical legislators to be absent from the scene at the time their countrymen were at last ready to try for the more effective union which both had painfully perceived as a necessity from their European observation posts. Within a few days of receiving copies of the Constitution, each hastened to write the other his initial reactions. Adams wrote on November 10, 1787. (Boyd, *Jefferson Papers,* XII, 335.)]

IT SEEMS to be admirably calculated to preserve the Union, to increase Affection, and to bring us all to the same mode of thinking. They have adopted the Idea of the Congress at Albany in 1754 of a President to nominate officers and a Council to Consent: but thank heaven they have adopted a third Branch, which that Congress did not. I think that Senates and Assemblies should have nothing to do with executive Power. But still I hope the Constitution will be adopted, and Amendments be made at a more convenient opportunity.

What think you of a Declaration of Rights? Should not such a Thing have preceded the Model?

[Jefferson's first thoughts to Adams were expressed on November 13. (Boyd, *Jefferson Papers,* XII, 350–51.)]

How DO you like our new constitution? I confess there are things in it which stagger all my dispositions to subscribe to what such an assembly has proposed. The house of federal representatives will not be adequate to the management of affairs either foreign or federal. Their President seems a bad edition of a Polish king. He may be reelected from 4. years to 4. years for life. Reason and experience prove to us that a chief magistrate, so continuable, is an officer for life. When one or two generations shall have proved that this is an office for life, it becomes on every succession worthy of intrigue, of bribery, of force, and even of foreign interference. It will be of great consequence to France and England to have America governed by a Galloman or Angloman. Once in office, and possessing the military force of the union, without either the aid or check of a council, he would not be easily dethroned, even if the people could be induced to withdraw their votes from him. I wish that at the end of the 4. years they had made him for ever ineligible a second time. Indeed I think all the good of this new constitution might have been couched in three or four new articles to be added to the good, old, and venerable fabrick, which should have been preserved even as a religious relique.

[Adams did little to bridge the disagreement between himself and Jefferson; on the contrary, he rose to the battle signal in his characteristic style of righteous (or self-righteous) candor. (C. F. Adams, *Works*, VIII, 464–65.)]

You ARE afraid of the one—I, of the few. We agree perfectly that the many should have a full fair and perfect Representation,—You are Apprehensive of Monarchy; I, of Aristocracy. I would therefore have given more Power to the President and less to the Senate. The Nomination and Appointment to all offices I would have given to the President, assisted only by a Privy Council of his own Creation, but not a Vote or Voice would I have given to the Senate or any Senator, unless he were of the Privy Council. Faction and Distraction are the sure and certain Consequence of giving to a Senate a vote in the distribution of offices.

You are apprehensive the President when once chosen, will be chosen again and again as long as he lives. So much the better as it appears to me.—You are apprehensive of foreign Interference, Intrigue, Influence. So am I.—But, as often as Elections happen, the danger of foreign Influence recurs. The less frequently they happen the less danger.—And if the Same Man may be chosen again, it is probable he will be, and the danger of foreign Influence will be less. Foreigners, seeing little Prospect will have less Courage for Enterprize.

Elections, my dear sir, Elections to offices which are great objects of Ambition, I look at with terror. Experiments of this kind have been so often tryed, and so universally found productive of Horrors, that there is great Reason to dread them.

[The two men continued to correspond, but they did not pursue the subject of the Constitution nor of the underlying philosophy of their divergent criticisms of it.]

*IV*

# ESTRANGEMENT: 1790's

## *A.*

### DIALOGUE ON MONARCHY

THE CLIMAX OF THE POLITICAL DISAGREEMENTS BETWEEN ADAMS AND Jefferson took place in May 1789, under the new government. The first issue which arose in the First Congress, when it met in New York, concerned the inauguration of the president and his future title. Madison reported to Jefferson that "a truly republican simplicity" had been adopted as the proper mode of address. He was, and henceforth would be called, "George Washington, President of the United States." Madison said that the House of Representatives had "spontaneously" accepted the constitutional title, but that the Senate had had to have this procedure "extorted" from them. He wrote that the question "became a serious one between the two houses. J. Adams espoused the cause of titles with great earnestness. His friend R. H. Lee altho elected as a republican enemy to an aristocratic constitution was a most zealous second. The projected title was—His Highness the President of the U.S. and protector of their liberties. Had the project succeeded it would have subjected the President to a severe dilemma and given a deep wound to our infant government." (Gaillard Hunt, ed., *The Writings of James Madison*, 9 vols. [New York: Putnam, 1900-10], V, 370.)

Jefferson's reaction to this information bore no trace of friendly indulgence for Adams. It was written in a mood of exasperation that undoutedly represented the cumulative strain of the preceding years. (Ford, *Writings of Jefferson*, V, 104)]

THE PRESIDENT's title as proposed by the senate was the most superlatively ridiculous thing I ever heard of. It is a proof the more of the justice of the character given by Doctr. Franklin of my friend: 'Always an honest man, often a great one, but sometimes absolutely mad.' I wish he could have been here during the late scenes [storming the Bastille, popular uprisings in Paris and the countryside]. If he could then have had one fibre of aristocracy left in his frame he would have been a proper subject for bedlam.

[The "divine science of politics" had lost the music of sweet speech. Greater disharmonies were to develop when both men were influential in the new nation in the decade of the 1790's. Even the most summary treatment of the events in that decade and the break between the two former friends would take us too far afield. For our purposes, it is enough to know, for now, that political differences that would lead to a break already existed. The gravity of the existing differences, already implicit in the political treatises they published while abroad and in their correspondence on the new Constitution, is made explicit in their correspondence to others on the issue of reconciling republicanism with monarchy.

A sequence of letters from Adams to his old and firm republican friend, Benjamin Rush, in the summer of 1789 is evidence of Adams' political mood at this time. A selection from one of them will serve to suggest the tenor of his political belief. (*Old Family Letters: Copied from the Originals for Alexander Biddle* [Philadelphia, 1892], pp. 37–38.)]

THAT EVERY Part of the Conduct and feelings of the Americans tends to that species of Republick called a limited Monarchy I agree. They were born and brought up in it. Their Habits are fixed in it: but their Heads are most miserably bewildered about it. There is not a more ridiculous Spectacle in the Universe than the Politicks of our Country exhibits: bawling about Republicanism which they understand not; and acting a Farce of Monarchy. We will have as you say "but one great Man" yet even he shall not be a great Man.

I also, am as much a Republican as I was in 1775. I do not "consider hereditary Monarchy or Aristocracy as Rebellion against Nature." On the contrary I esteem them both Institutions of admirable wisdom and exemplary Virtue in a certain stage of Society in a great Nation. The only Institutions that can possibly preserve the Laws and Liberties of the People, and I am clear that America must resort to them as an Asylum against Discord, Seditions and Civil War, and that at no very distant Period of time. I shall not live to see it—but you may. I think it therefore impolitick to cherish prejudices against Institutions which must be kept in view as the hope of our Posterity. I am by no means for attempting any such thing at present. Our Country is not ripe for it in many respects, and it is not yet necessary, but our ship must ultimately land on that shore or be cast away.

I do not "abhor Titles, nor the Pageantry of Government." If I did I should abhor Government itself: for there never was, and never will be, because there never can be, any Government without Titles and Pageantry. There is not a Quaker Family in Pensilvania, governed without Titles and Pageantry: not a school, not a colledge, not a club can be governed without them.

"I love the People," with you—too well to cheat them, lie to them or deceive them. I wish those who have flattered them so much had loved them half as well. If I had not loved them I never would have served them—if I did not love them now, I would not serve them another hour—for I very well know that vexation and Chagrine, must be my Portion, every moment I shall continue in public Life.

My Country appears to me I assure you in great danger of fatal Divisions, and especially because I scarcely know of two Persons, who think, speak and act alike, in matters of Government.

[Other letters in this sequence reveal that Adams thought his arguments were *in behalf of* "republican systems." The definition of a "republic" that he employed indicates how he could harbor such belief. As he stated in a letter on June 19, 1789, "Every Government that has more than one Man in its sovereignty is a republican system." He even admonished Rush: "You seem determined not to allow a limited monarchy to be a republican system, which it certainly is, and the best that has ever been tryed."

For Adams, then, there was a special brand of "realism" which placed the outward symbols of authority as high if not higher than reason and the reasonable compromises that would yield justice. To him, *all* governments, overtly or covertly, employed titles and ranks, degrees and orders, external display, and ceremony to awe the governed and hold them in lawful obedience. "Miracles will not be wrought for us. We don't deserve them," Adams bluntly, and truly, asserted. "In short," he announced, "Government is nothing else but Titles, Ceremonies and Ranks. They alone enable Reason to produce Justice."

For Jefferson, however, republicanism could never be made consistent with monarchy—limited or otherwise. France had been a laboratory in which the vices of monarchy had proven themselves fatal. He was so deeply committed to the vision of human freedom that kings and hereditary nobles, as symbols of an exalted power that degraded common people, were the conspicuous objects of his hatred. Jefferson had occasion to express this sentiment against monarchy when he was writing his numerous and detailed letters of comment on the proposed federal constitution. He had taken umbrage, as we may recall, at the possibility of a man's perpetual re-eligibility to the presidency. He had gone far beyond this point of criticism, of course, in his comprehensive letters to Madison. But to Washington, whose anti-monarchist beliefs Jefferson fully understood, he formulated a sweeping statement of his own judgment on kings. (Ford, *Writings of Jefferson*, V, 8.)]

I was much an enemy to monarchy before I came to Europe. I am ten thousand times more so since I have seen what they are. There is scarcely an evil known in these countries which may not be traced to their kings as its source, nor a good which is not derived from the small fibres of republicanism among them. I can further say with safety there is not a crowned head in Europe whose talents or merit would entitle him to be elected vestryman by the people of any parish in America.

[Only if it is understood that the absolutism of Jefferson's day and the corralling of total power into the hands of a government that ruled over the people were what he meant by monarchy—a system which made "the abusive state of man" the substitute for his natural and improved potentialities—can the intensity of his feelings be appreciated.

When Jefferson left France in 1789 and landed in Virginia, he was received enthusiastically by his neighbors. An official welcome had been prepared for him and was tendered by the "citizens of Albemarle County," hailing his past services to his country, both at home and abroad, and expressing the hope that he would continue to serve America. The "hope" was a civilized way of urging Jefferson to accept the position of Secretary of State which his neighbors knew he might not wish to undertake. Jefferson's reply, while it did not contain barbed sentences on monarchy, was the culmination of his deepest political faith as he entered upon more than a decade of political leadership and power. (Boyd, *Jefferson Papers*, XVI, 178–79.)]

THE TESTIMONY of esteem with which you are pleased to honour my return to my native county fills me with gratitude and pleasure. While it shews that my absence has not lost me your friendly recollection, it holds out the comfortable hope that when the hour of retirement shall come, I shall again find myself amidst those with whom I have long lived, with whom I wish to live, and whose affection is the source of my purest happiness. Their favor was the door thro' which I was ushered on the stage of public life; and while I have been led on thro' its varying scenes, I could not be unmindful of those who assigned me my first part.

My feeble and obscure exertions in their service, and in the holy cause of freedom, have had no other merit than that they were my best. We have all the same. We have been fellow-labourers and fellow-sufferers, and heaven has rewarded us with a happy issue from our struggles. It rests now with ourselves alone to enjoy in peace and concord the blessings of self-government, so long denied to mankind: to shew by example the sufficiency of human reason for the care of human affairs and that the will of the majority, the Natural law of every society, is the only sure guardian of the rights of man. Perhaps even this may sometimes err. But its errors are honest, solitary and short-lived.—Let us then, my dear friends, for ever bow down to the general reason of the society. We are safe with that, even in its deviations, for it soon returns again to the right way. These are lessons we have learnt together. We have prospered in their practice, and the liberality with which you are pleased to approve my attachment to the general rights of mankind assures me we are still together in these its kindred sentiments.

Wherever I may be stationed, by the will of my country, it will be my delight to see, in the general tide of happiness, that yours too flows on in just place and measure. That it may flow thro all times, gathering strength as it goes, and spreading the happy influence of reason and liberty over the face of the earth, is my fervent prayer to heaven.

[This background may partly explain the fact that when Jefferson (whom Mrs. Adams had christened in Europe "one of the choice ones of the earth") arrived in New York in 1790 to enter upon his duties as Secretary of State, there was not an enthusiastic reunion between him and Vice President Adams. In a set of notes on this period, Jefferson stated emphatically that he was dismayed by the political conversation at social gatherings which included the highest members of the government and their friends. Jefferson wrote that when he arrived in New York, President Washington received him cordially, as did his colleagues and their circle of friends. (Koch and Peden, *Jefferson*, pp. 120–21.)]

THE COURTESIES of dinner parties given me, as a stranger newly arrived among them, placed me at once in their familiar society. But I cannot describe the wonder and mortification with which the table conversations filled me. Politics were the chief topic, and a preference of kingly over republican government was evidently the favorite sentiment. An apostate I could not be, nor yet a hypocrite; and I found myself, for the most part, the only advocate on the republican side of the question, unless among the guests there chanced to be some member of that party from the legislative Houses.

[The summation of Jefferson's view of those two markedly different political tendencies was that they gave rise to the two major parties which emerged in the 1790's. He maintained much later in life and unquestionably also felt at the time that "the contests of that day were contests of principle, between the advocates of republican, and those of kingly government, and that had not the former made the efforts they did, our government would have been, even at this early day, a very different thing from what the successful issue of those efforts have made it." We have seen that Jefferson had already been apprised by Madison of Adams' role on the issue of titles for the president and high officials in the new government. He was now shortly to take alarm more from Hamilton's political views and practice than from Adams'.

But the irksome fact was that, while Jefferson recognized appreciable differences in doctrine and vast differences in character between the two Federalists, Adams by his lights had no choice but to uphold as vigorously as he could the executive power. The Vice President may have had private distaste for certain features of the Hamiltonian financial program (he had always inveighed against Avarice as the potential ruin of America, and speculators and profiteers were loathsome to him), but he exercised his deciding vote in the Senate at least twenty times in the course of the first Congress, upholding every phase of Hamilton's financial program and indeed all the measures that the Federalist side supported. Although Adams had entered office with the comment to his wife that "My country has in its wisdom contrived for me the most insignificant office that ever the invention of man contrived or his imagination conceived," he disproved the nullity of the office in unmistakable terms.

Jefferson, therefore, could hardly draw the distinction he might have liked between a good and worthy patriot who was his friend and a political opponent. Nonetheless, Jefferson did not assimilate the thought, the political ability, or the political behavior of Adams to that of Hamilton. An effort to formulate the significant differences between the two occurs in Jefferson's account of a Cabinet conference in Washington's first administration, which apparently made an indelible impression on him. (Koch and Peden, *Jefferson*, pp. 126–27.)]

. . . I WILL relate an anecdote, for the truth of which I attest the God who made me. Before the President set out on his southern tour in April, 1791, he addressed a letter . . . to the Secretaries of State, Treasury and War, desiring that if any serious and important cases should arise during his absence, they would consult and act on them. And he requested that the Vice President should also be consulted. This was the only occasion on which that officer was ever requested to take part in a cabinet question. Some occasion for consultation arising, I invited those gentlemen . . . to dine with me, in order to confer on the subject. After the cloth was removed, and our question agreed and dismissed, conversation began on other matters, and by some circumstance, was led to the British constitution, on which Mr. Adams observed, 'purge that constitution of its corruption, and give to its popular branch equality of representation, and it would be the most perfect constitution ever devised by the wit of man.' Hamilton paused and said, 'purge it of its corruption, and give to its popular branch equality of representation, and it would become an *impracticable* government: as it stands at present, with all its supposed defects, it is the most perfect government which ever existed.' And this was assuredly the exact line which separated the political creeds of these two gentlemen. The one was for two hereditary branches and an honest elective one; the other, for an hereditary King, with a House of Lords and Commons corrupted to his will, and standing between him and the people.

[In the same context, Jefferson further commented on Adams. (Koch and Peden, *Jefferson*, pp. 126–27.)]

MR. ADAMS had originally been a republican. The glare of royalty and nobility during his mission to England, had made him believe their fascination a necessary ingredient in government; and Shay's rebellion, not sufficiently understood where he then was, seemed to prove that the absence of want and oppression, was not a sufficient guarantee of order. His book on the American constitutions having made known his political bias, he was taken up by the monarchical federalists in his absence, and on his return to the United States, he was by then made to believe that the general disposition of our citizens was favorable to monarchy.

## B.

## DIALOGUE ON THE FRENCH REVOLUTION

❰The first arresting and authoritative voice to be raised in public in the United States against the French Revolution and its ideology was that of the Vice President. In April 1790, at just about the time when Jefferson arrived in New York to join the government, Adams wrote a curious letter to Dr. Richard Price. Dr. Price was a staunch English friend of liberty and of France, and in November 1789, before the London Revolution Society on the anniversary of the Glorious Revolution of 1688 in England, he delivered a sermon in which he voiced thanks to God for the privilege of being alive to see "30 millions of people spurning at slavery and demanding liberty with an irresistible voice." To this same learned dissenting minister whose political creed was an absolute brand of liberal natural rights, Adams made some scorching observations on the Revolution in France. He first called attention to his own support of similar sentiments to those expressed in Dr. Price's sermon, "On the Love of Country," saying he had served the cause of liberty from "the year 1760 to this hour" and at incalculable sacrifice of himself and his family. (C. F. Adams, *Works*, IX, 563–64.)]

THE REVOLUTION in France could not therefore be indifferent to me; but I have learned by awful experience to rejoice with trembling. I know that encyclopedists and economists, Diderot and D'Alembert, Voltaire and Rousseau, have contributed to this great event more than Sidney, Locke, or Hoadley, perhaps more than the American revolution; and I own to you, I know not what to make of a republic of thirty million atheists. The [French] Constitution is but an experiment, and must and will be altered. I know it to be impossible that France should be long governed by it. If the sovereignty is to reside in one assembly, the king, princes, of the blood, and principal quality, will govern it at their pleasure as long as they can agree; when they differ, they will go to war, and act over again all the tragedies of Valois, Bourbons, Lorraines, Guises, and Colignis, two hundred years ago. . . . Too many Frenchmen, after the example of too many Americans, pant for equality of persons and property. The impracticability of this, God Almighty has decreed, and the advocates for liberty, who attempt it, will surely suffer for it.

[He concluded this letter by reporting on affairs in America, thereby suggesting again a connection between the progress of the events upon which he had just rendered judgment and those at home. He delivered his opinion on the American experiment in an irascible tone, saying that only a tiny handful of people in any nation understood principles of government and that it was almost impossible to unite those few. He himself was a sincere inquirer after truth "but I find very few who discover the same truths." However, according to *his* lights, America would face its own difficulties: "Our new government is an attempt to divide a sovereignty; a fresh essay at *imperium in imperio*. It cannot, therefore, be expected to be very stable or very firm. It will prevent us for a time from drawing our swords upon each other, and when it will do that no longer, we must call a new Convention to reform it." (C. F. Adams, *Works*, IX, 563–64.)

This pattern of thought was substantially what inspired and shaped the series of essays, "Discourses on Davila," which Adams began to publish weekly in the columns of the *Gazette of the United States*. Adams submitted thirty-two essays from April 1790 until April 21, 1791. "The Discourses on Davila" were in part the translation of a book by Enrico Caterino Davila, *History of The Civil Wars of France*. First published in Venice in 1630, the *History* depicted the rivalries, intrigues, and bloody battles which formed the texture of events in France for the second half of the sixteenth century. Adams viewed this period of civil wars as an "instructive though melancholy history," warning that what had afflicted France in the sixteenth century prefigured the situation of France in 1791.

What Adams hoped to achieve by the unsystematic mass of essays was a fresh assault on the folly of liberty without balance and equality without the use of a privileged élite. In monitory tones, Adams issued the injunction: "Let the rich and the poor unite in the bands of mutual affection, be mutually sensible of each other's ignorance, weakness, and error, and unite in concerting measures for their mutual defence against each other's vices and follies, by supporting an impartial mediator." The people would be duped, he felt, unless it was taken as "certain" that emulation between individuals and rivalries among families "never can be prevented . . . ought not to be prevented, but directed to virtue, and then stimulated and encouraged by generous applause and honorable rewards." From this he drew the conclusion that "an effectual control be provided in the constitution, to check their excesses and balance their weights." Difficult though it might be to maintain the balance, it alone would guard the people from becoming so worried by rivalries that "from feeling, not from reasoning" they would set up a master and a despot for a protector.

From the violence of the history he had chosen to translate and present and from the preoccupation with nobility, great families, power-seeking and powerful individuals, it was easy to read the "Discourses" as an anti-republican philippic. It was certainly a large part of his intention to expose the French Revolution as doomed to failure, and he could easily be interpreted as meaning that any democratic republic was also doomed, that an environment that pretended to abolish aristocratic families was a cheat.

As soon as Jefferson arrived on the scene of goverment, he was concerned about the fact that news of the French Revolution was uniformly portrayed in the American press via hostile English sources.

He immediately arranged to have John Fenno, editor of the *Gazaette of the United States*, accept printing of government statutes and such foreign news as, in his view, would give a more objective account of European developments. On the basis of this arrangement, Jefferson supplied news of the French Revolution from the *Leyden Gazette* which was distinctly sympathetic to French developments, and as early as 1790 a selection from one of Edmund Burke's speeches in Parliament attacking the French Revolution appeared. This was about the time when Adams' "Discourses on Davila" began to appear.

Meanwhile in England, Burke's *Reflections on the French Revolution* had been issued in November 1790, and Paine's reply to Burke's attack, in the shape of the first volume of *The Rights of Man*, was printed early in 1791. In London, where the latter appeared, it caused a sensation, selling furiously and alarming the British government to the point where it attempted to suppress the work and prosecute its author, the printer, and the distributors. One scholar summed up this great controversy in which Burke and Paine were the principal antagonists as "perhaps the most crucial ideological debate ever carried on in English." (Thomas Copeland in *Edmund Burke: Six Essays* [New Haven: Yale Univ. Press, 1949], p. 148.)

When Paine's volume was about to appear in America, a copy was loaned to Jefferson who then transmitted it to the publisher with a fateful note. He meant the note to be private, for in it he expressed his satisfaction that Paine's work would be reprinted in the United States and "that something is at length to be publicly said against the political heresies which have sprung up among us." The publisher avidly seized on this note as a recommendation for the volume and printed it over Jefferson's title as Secretary of State. Whose heresies were intended? The public at once took the note as a denunciation of Adams and his notorious "Davila" pieces. Again the Paine volume created a furor when it appeared, for now there were two highly-placed antagonists—the Secretary of State and the Vice President—for the public to watch. To heighten the spectacle, Paine had dedicated his volume to the President, George Washington (he had originally scheduled his book to be published on Washington's birthday).

Jefferson was appalled when he discovered that the note had been printed and hastened to make explanations to various key people. To several of his correspondents, including Washington, he admitted that he had referred to Adams' "apostacy to hereditary monarchy and nobility." Indeed to Madison, Jefferson confessed that he "had in view certainly the doctrines of Davila" and their pro-British sentiments. What he said with equal truth to Madison and everyone else was that he never intended to have his note printed and that he had just reason to think Adams "will be displeased"—a small word, as Jefferson must have known, for the expectable reaction.

Finally he wrote to Adams explaining how the note had been published against his wishes and declaring "in the presence of the almighty that nothing was further from my intention or expectation than to have had either my own or your name brought before the public on this occasion. That you and I differ in our ideas of the best form of government is well known to us both," he added, "but we have differed as friends should do, respecting the purity of each other's motives, and confining our difference of opinion to private conversation."

Adams had to accept Jefferson's explanation of the circumstances under which the note had appeared, but he bridled at one part of Jefferson's letter. (C. F. Adams, *Works*, VIII, 506–9.)]

YOU OBSERVE, "that you and I differ in our ideas of the best form of government, is well known to us both." But, my dear Sir, you will give me leave to say that I do not know this. I know not what your idea is of the best form of government. You and I have never had a serious conversation together, that I can recollect, concerning the nature of government. The very transient hints that have ever passed between us have been jocular and superficial, without ever coming to an explanation. If you suppose that I have, or ever had, a design or desire of attempting to introduce a government of King, Lords, and Commons, or in other words, an hereditary executive, or an hereditary senate, either into the government of the United States or that of any individual State, you are wholly mistaken. There is not such a thought expressed or intimated in any public writing or private letter, and I may safely challenge all mankind to produce such a passage, and quote the chapter and verse. If you have ever put such a construction on any thing of mine, I beg you would mention it to me, and I will undertake to convince you, that it has no such meaning. Upon this occasion I will venture to say that my unpolished Writings, although they have been read by a sufficient Number of Persons to have assisted in crushing the Insurrection of the Massachusetts, in the formation of the new Constitution of Pennsylvania, Georgia and South Carolina, and in procuring the Assent of all the States to the new national Constitution, yet they have not been read by great Numbers. Of the few who have taken the pains to read them, some have misunderstood them and others have wilfully misrepresented them, and those misunderstandings and misrepresentations have been made the pretence for overwhelming me with floods and Whirlwinds of tempestuous Abuse, unexampled in the History of this Country. . . .

I thank you, Sir, very sincerely for writing to me upon this Occasion. It was high time that you and I should come to an explanation with each other. The friendship that has subsisted for fifteen Years between Us without the smallest interruption, and until this occasion without the slightest Suspicion, ever has been and still is, very dear to my heart. There is no office which I would not resign, rather than give a just occasion to one friend to forsake me. Your motives for writing to me, I have not a doubt were the most pure and the most friendly; and I have no suspicion that you will not receive this explanation from me in the same candid Light. . . .

[The correspondence languished thenceforth, and the two erstwhile friends found it impossible to discuss the developing political issues confronting the new Republic in a frank and searching way.

At this point, we might pause to ask what it was that had produced the growing coolness between the two men. One possibility is that they had been more opposed all along in fundamental political principles than they had realized. In what sense did Adams believe in "monarchy" and "aristocracy," and did this mean that he was not a "republican" as Jefferson used the term? Another possibility is that alarm over the French Revolution had caused a basic change in Adams' ideas on these points. Does the Adams of the "Davila" period seem to you less of a "republican" than the Adams of the earlier writings? A final possibility is that any change in Adams' thinking was more apparent than real. Perhaps revolution abroad and rising party strife at home had pushed him temporarily into making statements that were more extreme than he intended without changing the underlying structure of his thought. Which of these possibilities seems most consistent with the evidence you have read?

## C.

### PARTY OPPOSITION AND "SEDITION"

❡The mounting party battle was transforming the coolness between Jefferson and Adams into outright enmity. Irritation with Hamilton's program and Hamilton's domination of the administration caused Jefferson to resign from Washington's cabinet in 1793, and, when party conflict reached its peak in 1795 in the debate over Jay's treaty with England, Jefferson had come to be regarded as the leader of the Republican opposition. The next year Adams and Jefferson were pitted against each other as their respective parties' candidates for president to succeed Washington. Jefferson ran only three votes behind Adams in the electoral college and, under the electoral system prevailing at that time, became Vice President.

Briefly in the early days of the Adams administration, it seemed that the old cordiality between the two men might be restored. Instead a crisis in the country's relations with France brought their personal estrangement to its most acrimonious stage. When the French foreign minister, Talleyrand, in the famous XYZ correspondence, demanded bribes before he would treat with the American commissioners over French depredations on American shipping, Adams threw himself into the hands of Hamilton's High Federalists and beat the drums for war. As the undeclared naval war began, the Federalist press obtained and printed a private letter Jefferson had written to Philip Mazzei, the Italian historian who had once been his neighbor in Virginia. In this letter Jefferson declared that "an Anglican, monarchical & aristocratical party has sprung up, whose avowed object is to draw over us the substance as they have already done the forms of the British government. . . . It would give you a fever were I to name to you the apostates who have gone over to these heresies, men who were Samsons in the field & Solomons in the council, but who have had their heads shorn by the harlot England." (Ford, *Writings of Jefferson*, VII, 75–76.)

Meanwhile, in private correspondence, Jefferson had been terming Adams' French policy "almost insane." Learning of Jefferson's criticism, Adams lashed back: "It is evidence of a mind, soured, yet seeking for popularity, and eaten to a honeycomb with ambition, yet weak, confused, uninformed and ignorant." (C. F. Adams, *Works of Adams*, VIII, 546–47.)

Under the pressures of the French crisis, Congress and the Adams administration introduced measures to promote national security as they saw it. One set of measures concerned the defense establishment. The Department of the Navy was established and naval appropriations were increased to begin a building program under the direct instigation of the President, and the army was increased.

Under the guise of national security, a second and more fateful set of measures was adopted during the Adams administration. In June and July of 1798, the Federalists pushed through Congress acts designed to inhibit the growth and effectiveness of political opposition. The targets were the friends and foreign born adherents of the Republican party, the Republican press, and free speech. These repressive measures were offered under the pretext of war measures, although there was no formal declaration of war and the "quasi-war" with France on the seas was not different in kind, though different in degree at this time, from previous British depredations on American shipping. These acts were not sent up to Congress by the President, but nevertheless Adams signed the legislation and Hamilton, who had written one letter when the legislation was first proposed urging that Federalists in Congress be careful not to impose tyranny, approved the legislation which emerged and soon called for more vigorous execution than Adams was inclined to employ.

The Naturalization Act changed the period of residence for admission to citizenship from five to fourteen years. The intent was clearly to halt the recruitment of new immigrant voters by the Republican party and to put a lid on radical and reforming Irish, English, and French immigrants. The Alien Act gave the government the power to deport or arrest all aliens in the country, and Jefferson immediately believed it was aimed at men like Gallatin, the Swiss-born leader of the Republicans in Congress (who would be judged by John Adams' great-grandson, Henry Adams, as a man of superb talents, suited to become president of the United States), and Volney, the French philosopher and friend of Jefferson who resided in Philadelphia for three years gathering materials for his book on the geography of the United States and Indian vocabulary. Dr. Joseph Priestley, the famous chemist and theologian, had been forced to leave England and arrived in Philadelphia just in time to be threatened with deportation. Adams was embarrassed to enforce the order in Priestley's case (despite fervid requests from Secretary of State Pickering) because he had been Priestley's friend in London, had corresponded with him in the intervening years, and had enjoyed and attended his sermons frequently. But Priestley was a closer friend of Jefferson and shared the liberal views of the Republicans.

The third major law was popularly known as the Sedition Act. It passed the House of Representatives by a narrow margin of forty-four to forty-one, with all but two of the majority representing the North. This act made verbal or written attacks on the government, its officers, and policies criminal libels triable by Federal courts, and it was specifically designed to repress political opposition and to halt the Republican presses. The prime and immediate target was the Philadelphia *Aurora*, then under the editorship of Franklin's grandson, Benjamin Franklin Bache (none too affectionately called "Lightning Rod, Jr."). Bache cheated the Federalists of a sedition prosecution by dying of yellow fever in September 1798. His successor, William Duane, who pledged himself to Bache's principles, became the new candidate for Federalist harassment. Under the Sedition Act, the five leading Jeffersonian journals—the Philadelphia *Aurora*, the Boston *Independent Chronicle*, the New York *Argus*, the Richmond *Examiner*, and the Baltimore *American* —were selected for punishment. Suits were brought against all except the Baltimore *American*, and the editors of four other pro-Republican newspapers of smaller circulation were indicted. Ten Republican editors were subsequently convicted, among them James Callender; William Duane; and the philosopher, scholar, and friend of Priestley and Jefferson, Thomas Cooper. The moving spirits in these trials were Secretary of State Pickering as chief enforcement officer and Justice Samuel Chase of the United States Supreme Court.

Adams defended these laws in public speeches and helped enforce them in what he considered to be a "strict interpretation" rather than a loose one. Five days after he had signed the sedition bill into law, he said in one of his addresses, "Until lately licentiousness has been too little restrained." Presumably restraint would now be exerted. A few weeks later, he replied to the citizens of Boston "that the profligate spirit of falsehood and malignity, which has appeared in some, and the unguarded disposition in others, to encourage it, are serious evils, and bear a threatening aspect upon the Union of the State, their Constitution of Government, and the moral character of the Nation." About a month later, in a New York address, Adams endorsed the sentiments that motivated the Alien law, cautioning about the influx of foreigners, of discontented characters in the United States. "If we glory in making our country an asylum for virtue in distress and for innocent industry, it behoves us to beware, that under this pretext it is not made a receptacle of malevolence and turbulence, for the outcasts of the universe." Most revealing of the length to which Adams would go against free inquiry—and curiously ironic in its bearings on the contribution of the DuPont family to economic growth in America—is his letter to Secretary of State Pickering. (C. F. Adams, *Works*, VIII, 596.)]

I SHALL not be guilty of so much affection of regard to science, as to be very willing to grant passports to Dupont de Nemours or any other French philosophers, in the present situations of our country. We have had too many French philosophers already, and I really begin to think, or rather to suspect, that learned academies, not under the immediate inspection and control of government, have disorganized the world, and are incompatible with social order.

[Jefferson, on the other hand, was dismayed by the betrayal of liberty which he saw in these measures. As soon as the bills were presented to Congress, he wrote to Madison. (Ford, *Writings of Jefferson*, VII, 266–67.)]

THEY [the Federalists] have brought into the lower house a sedition bill, which among other enormities, undertakes to make printing certain matters criminal, tho' one of the amendments to the Constitution has so expressly taken religion, printing presses &c. out of their coercion. Indeed this bill and the alien bill both are so palpably in the teeth of the Constitution as to show they mean to pay no respect to it.

[Jefferson's opposition was avowedly based on two grounds. One was philosophical. This philosophical view was expressed in June 1799, when he wrote to a college student, William Green Munford. (June 18, 1799, Manuscript letter, Teachers College Library, Columbia University.)]

I JOIN you . . . in branding as cowardly the idea that the human mind is incapable of further advances. This is precisely the doctrine which the present despots of the earth are inculcating, and their friends here re-echoing; and applying especially to religion and politics: 'that it is not probable that anything better will be discovered than what was known to our fathers.' We are to look backwards then and not forwards for the improvement of science, and to find it amidst feudal barbarisms and the fires of Spital-fields. But thank heaven the American mind is already too much opened, to listen to these impostures; and while the art of printing is left to us, science can never be retrograde; what is once acquired of real knowledge can never be lost. To preserve the freedom of the human mind then and freedom of the press, every spirit should be ready to devote itself to martyrdom; for as long as we may think as we will, and speak as we think the condition of man will proceed in improvement. The generation which is going off the stage has deserved well of mankind for the struggles it has made, and for having arrested that course of despotism which had overwhelmed the world for thousands and thousands of years. If there seems to be danger that the ground they have gained will be lost again, that danger comes from the generation your contemporary. But that the enthusiasm which characterizes youth should lift its parricide hands against freedom and science would be such a monstrous phaenomenon as I can not place among possible things in this age and this country.

[The second ground for Jefferson's opposition was practical: to save his political life. He judged the war hysteria over the French crisis, whipped up to fever pitch by the Federalists, as the opportunity they would use to destroy the Republican opposition. In April 1798, he wrote to Madison about the passage of the various defense measures for the Army and Navy. "In this state of things they [Federalists] will carry what they please. One of the war party, in a fit of unguarded passion, declared some time ago they would pass a citizen bill, an alien bill, & a sedition bill. . . . But it will not stop there when it gets into a course of execution. . . . At present, the war hawks talk of septemberizing, Deportation, and the examples for quelling sedition set by the French Executive. All the firmness of the human mind is now in a state of requisition." But at this time, he still felt that the fever would pass, that the native Republican habits of the American people would defeat these usurpations if the country could stay out of war. Thus, in a letter to James Lewis a month later he commented. (Ford, *Writings of Jefferson,* VII, 205.)]

AT THIS moment all the passions are boiling over, and one who keeps himself cool and clear of the contagion, is so far below the point of ordinary conversation, that he finds himself insulated in every society. However, the fever will not last. War, land tax & stamp tax, are sedatives which must calm its ardor. They will bring on reflection, and that, with information is all which our countrymen need, to bring themselves and their affairs to rights. They are essentially republican. They retain unadulterated the principles of '75, and those who are conscious of no change in themselves have nothing to fear in the long run. It is our duty still to endeavor to avoid war; but if it shall actually take place, no matter by whom brought on, we must defend ourselves. If our house be on fire, without inquiring whether it was fired from within or without, we must try to extinguish it. In that, I have no doubt, we shall act as one man.

[As the Adams administration moved ahead with its defense, security, and tax programs there was increased discontent, increased criticism, and even talk of defiance and secession. For example, John Taylor of Caroline broached the idea of separation by Virginia and North Carolina from the union. Jefferson then firmly rejected this kind of speculative talk and urged patience. The burden of his argument was that "in every free and deliberating society, there must, from the nature of man, be opposite parties, and violent dissensions and discords; and one of these, for the most part, must prevail over the other for a longer or shorter time. Perhaps this party division is necessary to induce each to watch and delate the proceedings of the other to the people. But if on a temporary superiority of the one party, the other is to resort to a scission of the Union, no federal government can ever exist." Therefore, "A little patience, and we shall see the reign of witches pass over, their spells dissolved, and the people recovering their true sight, restoring their government to its true principles." (Ford, *Writings of Jefferson,* VII, 264–65.)
But "the reign of witches" did not end very soon or very easily. Jefferson suspected that he was under surveillance by Federalist spies, that his mail was being tampered with, that his friends were being

singled out for attack, and that he himself, as leader of the Republican "Jacobin puppets," might be charged with sedition. He felt that there was increasing evidence from all quarters of what we have now come to term "the police state." Under such circumstances his patience wore thin, and his reason could no longer remain cool. He saw that freedom everywhere in Europe was on the run and that the new American experiment in free society had reached a turning point. How could he effectively combat the presumption that criticism of the government was sedition? How could he effectively organize support for Republican principles to win the coming elections in 1800? Jefferson realized that Philadelphia was not the place to forward these plans. Therefore, even while the repressive legislation was before the Senate and knowing that its passage was a foregone conclusion, he returned to Virginia to formulate a counter-offensive.

It is against this background that one must view the work of Jefferson and Madison in secretly authoring and organizing the protests known as the Kentucky and Virginia Resolutions. These resolutions have proved to be a double-edged sword. On the one hand, they have been appealed to for the doctrine of states' rights and have been employed to deny human freedoms and weaken the federal government under the Constitution. But Jefferson and Madison, who were the authors, employed the logic of the compact theory of the federal government to extend human liberty and to protect free government. For them, the resolutions were measures of "solemn protest" against the repressive laws of the Adams administration, and they ended by soliciting the opinion of their "sister states."

This summary account of Adams and Jefferson as party opponents terminates with the victory of the Republicans in the election of 1800. Before Adams yielded office to Jefferson, however, two important developments took place which affected the relationship between the two men in the years that lay ahead. First, when Adams learned in 1799 from various sources (including reports from men he considered trustworthy, like William Vans Murray in Holland and Rufus King in England) that France was prepared for a reconciliation with America, he undertook, secretly and swiftly, to negotiate. He was convinced that high taxes in America boded only evil for domestic peace and order, and he had concluded that Hamilton's insistence on continuing hostilities against France and currying favor with Great Britain were the worst possible policy at the time. Hamilton, in a personal interview with the President, had acted, in Adams' judgment, as though he had had a special revelation from God that if the United States entered upon peace negotiations with France, the British would declare war upon the United States. Adams' comment on this interview was that "never in my life did I hear a man talk more like a fool." When Adams' peace commissioners successfully completed their negotiations with the French, Adams viewed this act of his administration as the most significant of his achievements. He wrote: "I desire no other inscription over my gravestone than: 'Here lies John Adams, who took upon himself the responsibility of the peace with France in the year 1800.'"

But, by the same deed, Hamilton saw the utter collapse of his ambitions for glory. Furious in his defeat, Hamilton retaliated. He slashed at Adams without mercy by writing a virulent attack on *The Public Conduct and Character of John Adams, Esq., President of the United States.* This piece of attempted character assassination appeared during the last week of October, too late to permit a reply before the presidential election of 1800 took place. It provided the country with the spectacle of the two most powerful Federalists in the nation—one the official candidate for the presidency, the other the experienced ex-statesman and party boss—locked in ugly and mortal combat. By this unpredictable route, Adams and Jefferson were brought to something resembling more similar ground than they had occupied in the decade of Federalist power. Both men had now openly battled with Hamilton, and both were now in agreement on the peace with France and prudent independence of Britain.

The second important development, however, opened new sources for Jefferson's resentment of Adams. After Jefferson's election was assured, the Federalist Congress made haste to convert the national judiciary into a Federalist stronghold against the victorious "Jacobins." By the Judiciary Act of 1801, which effected a complete reorganization and expansion of the federal judicial system, the outgoing president was permitted to make many appointments to new posts, including the naming of sixteen new circuit court judges. These were lifetime appointments; all of them went to Federalists, some of them men who had failed to obtain re-election to Congress. On the last day in office, at virtually the moment when he would have to surrender the seal of his office as President, Adams signed the commissions for these "midnight appointments." These, plus the appointment of John Marshall (a distant kinsman and longtime foe of Jefferson's) as Chief Justice were the ominous legacy Adams bequeathed to Jefferson. The Federalist strategy of devising this means to perpetuate itself regardless of the popular will had been partisan through and through, and Adams, in a bleak and angry mood, had played his part. Then, in the cold dawn of March 4, 1801, Adams made a hasty retreat from Washington just before Jefferson delivered his Inaugural Address to a crowded Senate chamber.

In the Address, Jefferson stated the sentiments in which he had long "and radically" believed. (Koch and Peden, *Jefferson,* pp. 321–23.)]

DURING THE contest of opinion through which we have passed, the animation of discussion and of exertions has sometimes worn an aspect which might impose on strangers unused to think freely and to speak and to write what they think; but this being now decided by the voice of the nation, announced according to the rules of the constitution, all will, of course, arrange themselves under the will of the law, and unite in common efforts for the common good. All, too, will bear in mind this sacred principle, that though the will of the majority is in all cases to prevail, that will, to be rightful, must be reasonable; that the minority possess their equal rights, which equal laws must protect, and to violate which would be oppression. Let us, then, fellow citizens, unite with one heart and one mind. Let us restore to social intercourse that harmony and affection without which liberty and even life itself are but dreary things. And let us reflect that having banished from our land that religious intolerance under which mankind so long bled and suffered, we have yet gained little if we countenance a political intolerance as despotic, as wicked, and capable of as bitter and bloody persecutions. During the throes and convulsions of the ancient world, during the agonizing spasms of infuriated man, seeking through blood and slaughter his long-lost liberty, it was not wonderful that the agitations of the billows should reach even this distant and peaceful shore; that this should be more felt and feared by some and less by others; that this should divide opinions as to measures of safety. But every difference of opinion is not a difference of principle. We have called by different names brethren of the same principle. We are all republicans—we are all federalists. If there be any among us who would wish to dissolve this Union or to change its republican form, let them stand undisturbed as monuments of the safety with which error of opinion may be tolerated where reason is left free to combat it. I know, indeed, that some honest men fear that a republican government cannot be strong; that this government is not strong enough. But would the honest patriot, in the full tide of successful experiment, abandon a government which has so far kept us free and firm, on the theoretic and visionary fear that this government, the world's best hope, may by possibility want energy to preserve itself? I trust not. I believe this, on the contrary, the strongest government on earth. I believe it is the only one where every man, at the call of the laws, would fly to the standard of the law, and would meet invasions of the public order as his own personal concern. Sometimes it is said that man cannot be trusted with the government of himself. Can he, then, be trusted with the government of others? Or have we found angels in the form of kings to govern him? Let history answer this question.

# REUNION IN RETIREMENT: 1812–1826

## *A.*

### THE FRIENDSHIP RESUMES

FOR THE LAST TWENTY-FIVE YEARS OF THEIR LIVES, ADAMS AND JEFFERSON never saw one another face to face, and from 1801 to 1812, not a single scrip of the pen was exchanged. To be sure, Mrs. Adams opened a round of correspondence in 1804 between herself and President Jefferson on the sad occasion of the death of his younger daughter, Maria, the beautiful little "Polly" who, years ago, had captured Abigail Adams' heart in London. But the friendship which they tried to grasp had surprisingly many drawbacks, and before long Mrs. Adams wrote firmly that she was closing the correspondence. She had mentioned two unkind deeds which she held against Jefferson: his donation of money to the "venomous" Callender, who had been jailed under the Sedition Act and who had been a particularly unendurable burr in Adams' side; and the removal of her son, John Quincy Adams, from his position as one of the commissioners of bankruptcy in the Boston area. On his part, Jefferson explained that Congressional action had closed her son's appointment, and this explanation she found valid. However, she could not condone Jefferson's leniency toward Callender in releasing him and remitting his fine. But neither could Jefferson forgive Adams for the "only act" that gave him "personal displeasure"—the "midnight appointments." Thus matters stood between Jefferson and the Adams family until Jefferson's friend and political collaborator, Madison, appointed John Quincy Adams to be the first American Minister to the court of Russia in 1809. By this step, John Adams' son, who could no more keep communion with a political party than could his father, entered a political future made bright by the Republicans. His exulting father, watching each step, found in the country's approval of his son partial easement for its "past" cruelty to himself.

No wonder then that Adams was prepared to listen when Benjamin Rush barraged him (and, as Adams suspected, "teased" Jefferson in the same way) with urgent entreaties that he and Jefferson, "fellow laborers in erecting the great fabric of American independence! . . .

embrace—embrace each other." Meanwhile, young Edward Coles, Madison's secretary, visited Adams and reported to Rush and Jefferson that Adams, in the flush of reminiscence and conversation, had said: "I always loved Jefferson, and still love him." At length Adams was on the point of yielding. He grumbled that there would be "no use" in exchanging letters; that "when there has been no war, there can be no room for negotiations of peace"—why so much ado about nothing? In a jesting tone that Adams specially cultivated, he protested that there never had been any substantial differences between Jefferson and himself. (Koch and Peden, *Adams*, pp. 165–66.)]

IN POINT of republicanism, all the difference I ever knew or could discover. . . . between Jefferson and me consisted,

1. In the difference between speeches and messages. I was a monarchist because I thought a speech more manly, more respectful to Congress and the nation. Jefferson . . . preferred messages.

2. I held levees once a week, that all my time might not be wasted by idle visits. Jefferson's whole eight years was a levee.

3. I dined a large company once or twice a week. Jefferson dined a dozen every day.

4. Jefferson and Rush were for liberty and straight hair. I thought curled hair was as republican as straight.

In these, and a few other points of equal importance, all miserable frivolities, that Jefferson and Rush ought to blush that they ever laid any stress upon them, I might differ; but I never knew any points of more consequence on which there was any variation between us.

[That was Christmas day, 1811. On the first day of the new year Adams wrote a self-conscious little note to the old friend from whom he had been estranged. Jefferson lost little time in sending an affectionate letter invoking memories of their earlier years together when "beset with difficulties and dangers, we were fellow laborers in the same cause." He then reviewed the "rubs and set-backs" which America had experienced—"in your day French depredations; in mine English, and the Berlin and Milan decrees: now the English order of council, and the piracies they authorise"—a list which deliberately put all the living presidents on a par. Then a priceless Jeffersonian touch: "and so we have gone on, and so we shall go on, puzzled and prospering beyond example in the history of man." (Koch and Peden, *Jefferson*, p. 616.)

Thus opened one of the most brilliant correspondences in American history: full of color and controversy, ideas and passionate pronouncements, people they had known—great and small who were in some way interesting, books and the whole vast tissue of Western learning, history in its deceits and in its glories, philosophy, religion, the truth—about man, society, themselves. Sometimes the comments were barbed, provocative, gleefully malicious on Adams' part; always they were played "straight" by Jefferson, as though he had not noted the innuendo, not felt the prod. Jefferson's art was to proceed firmly, graciously, and so smoothly that even a testy and egotistical man could be made to tolerate an unwelcome truth and to entertain opinion widely but gently critical of his own.

The correspondence which was their reunion reveals markedly different personalities. Adams was intensely personal, making history drama and melodrama. He was vain, endlessly self-justifying, full of shifting moods, and his prose crackled with the fresh language of his intractable spirit. He seemed naturally drawn to existential crises and absurdities, hungering for the ideal, while groaning about his fellow-pilgrims, yet, "I know not whether to laugh or to weep." Jefferson, on the other hand, was vividly intelligent and benign, harmonizing as he could the dictates of the head and heart. He reserved passionate eloquence for the causes he held sacred and for the few but fundamental hatreds which he felt bound to voice. Tyranny, the abuse of man, the confining of man's mind, hope, and search—to these he swore "eternal hostility."

The abundant correspondence of their late years shows Adams and Jefferson were in their own ways loyal to human excellence and human liberty. But did their visions of liberty differ? If so, how? Had they, indeed, only fought in the prime of their lives over mere "frivolities"—over straight versus curled hair? And, as you read the correspondence selected from their mellow older years, do you find them in substantial argreement or disagreement?]

*B.*

## DIALOGUE ON PARTIES

*Jefferson* (Koch and Peden, *Jefferson*, pp. 627–28.)

MEN HAVE differed in opinion, and been divided into parties by these opinions, from the first origin of societies; and in all governments where they have been permitted freely to think and to speak. The same political parties which now agitate the U.S. have existed thro' all time. Whether the power of the people, or that of the ["aristocrats"] should prevail, were questions which kept the states of Greece and Rome in eternal convulsions; as they now schismatize every people whose minds and mouths are not shut up by the gag of a despot. And in fact the terms of whig and tory belong to natural, as well as to civil history. They denote the temper and constitution of mind of different individuals. . . .

To me . . . it appears that there have been differences of opinion, and party differences, from the first establishment of governments, to the present day; and on the same question which now divides our own country: that these will continue thro' all future time: that every one takes his side in favor of the many, or of the few, according to his constitution, and the circumstances in which he is placed: that opinions, which are equally honest on both sides, should not affect personal esteem, or social intercourse: that as *we* judge between the Claudii and the Gracchi, the Wentworths and the Hampdens of past ages, so, of those among us whose names may happen to be remembered for awhile, the next generations will judge, favorably or unfavorably, according to the complexion of individual minds, and the side they shall themselves have taken: that nothing new can be added by you or me to what has been said by others, and will be said in every age, in support of the conflicting opinions on government: and that wisdom and duty dictate an humble resignation to the verdict of our future peers.

*Adams* (C. F. Adams, *Works*, X, 48.)

The real terrors of both Parties have allways been, and now are, The fear that they shall lose the Elections and consequently the Loaves and Fishes; and that their Antagonists will obtain them. Both parties have excited artificial Terrors and if I were summoned as a Witness to say upon Oath, which Party had excited, Machiavillialy, the most terror, and which had really felt the most, I could not give a more sincere Answer, than in the vulgar Style "Put Them in a bagg and shake them, and then see which comes out first."

## C.

## DIALOGUE ON ARISTOCRACY AND EQUALITY

⟨The two friends also held an absorbing, open-ended dialogue on aristocracy and equality. What does each mean by natural aristocracy? In what sense does each man believe in equality?⟩

*Jefferson* (Koch and Peden, *Jefferson*, pp. 632–34.)

I AGREE with you that there is a natural aristocracy among men. The grounds of this are virtue and talents. Formerly bodily powers gave place among the aristoi. But since the invention of gunpowder has armed the weak as well as the strong with missile death, bodily strength, like beauty, good humor, politeness and other accomplishments, has become but an auxiliary ground of distinction. There is also an artificial aristocracy founded on wealth and birth; without either virtue or talents; for with these it would belong to the first class. The natural aristocracy I consider as the most precious gift of nature for the instruction, the trusts, and government of society. And indeed it would have been inconsistent in creation to have formed man for the social state, and not to have provided virtue and wisdom enough to manage the concerns of the society. May we not even say that that form of government is the best which provides the most effectually for a pure selection of these natural aristoi into the offices of government? The artificial aristocracy is a mischievous ingredient in government, and provision should be made to prevent its ascendancy. On the question, What is the best provision, you and I differ; but we differ as rational friends, using the free exercise of our own reason, and mutually indulging it's errors. *You* think it best to put the pseudo-aristoi into a separate chamber of legislation where they may be hindered from doing mischief by their coordinate branches, and where also they may be a protection to wealth against the Agrarian and plundering enterprises of the Majority of the people. I think that to give them power in order to prevent them from doing mischief, is arming them for it, and increasing instead of remedying the evil. For if the coordinate branches can arrest their action, so may they that of the coordinates. Mischief may be done negatively as well as positively. Of this a cabal in the Senate of the U.S. has furnished many proofs. Nor do I believe them necessary to protect the wealthy; because enough of these will find their way into every branch of the legislation to protect themselves. From 15. to 20. legislatures of our own, in action for 30. years past, have proved that no fears of an equalisation of property are to be apprehended from them.

*I* think the best remedy is exactly that provided by all our constitutions, to leave to the citizens the free election and separation of the aristoi from the pseudo-aristoi, of the wheat from the chaff. In general they will elect the real good and wise. In some instances, wealth may corrupt, and birth blind them; but not in sufficient degree to endanger the society.

It is probable that our difference of opinion may in some measure be produced by a difference of character in those among whom we live. From what I have seen of Massachusets and Connecticut myself, and still more from what I have heard, and the character given of the former by yourself, who know them so much better, there seems to be in those two states a traditionary reverence for certain families, which has rendered the offices of the government nearly hereditary in those families. I presume that from an early period of your history, members of these families happening to possess virtue and talents, have honestly exercised them for the good of the people, and by their services have endeared their names to them. . . .

But altho' this hereditary succession to office with you may in some degree be founded in real family merit, yet in a much higher degree it has proceeded from your strict alliance of church and state. These families are canonised in the eyes of the people on the common principle 'you tickle me, and I will tickle you.' In Virginia we have nothing of this. Our clergy, before the revolution, having been secured against rivalship by fixed salaries, did not give themselves the trouble of acquiring influence over the people. Of wealth, there were great accumulations in particular families, handed down from generation to generation under the English law of entails. But the only object of ambition for the wealthy was a seat in the king's council. All their court then was paid to the crown and it's creatures; and they Philipised in all collisions between the king and people. Hence they were unpopular; and that unpopularity continues attached to their names. A Randolph, a Carter, or a Burwell must have great personal superiority over a common competitor to be elected by the people, even at this day. . . .

With respect to Aristocracy, we should further consider that, before the establishment of the American states, nothing was known to History but the Man of the old world, crouded within limits either small or over-charged, and steeped in the vices which that situation generates. A government adapted to such men would be one thing;

but a very different one that for the Man of these states. Here every one may have land to labor for himself if he chuses; or, preferring the exercise of any other industry, may exact for it such compensation as not only to afford a comfortable subsistence, but wherewith to provide for a cessation from labor in old age. Every one, by his property, or by his satisfactory situation, is interested in the support of law and order. And such men may safely and advantageously reserve to themselves a wholsome controul over their public affairs, and a degree of freedom, which in the hands of the Canaille of the cities of Europe, would be instantly perverted to the demolition and destruction of every thing public and private. The history of the last 25. years of France, and of the last 40. years in America, nay of it's last 200. years, proves the truth of both parts of this observation.

But even in Europe a change has sensibly taken place in the mind of Man. Science had liberated the ideas of those who read and reflect, and the American example had kindled feelings of right in the people. An insurrection has consequently begun, of science, talents and courage against rank and birth, which have fallen into contempt. It has failed in it's first effort, because the mobs of the cities, the instrument used for it's accomplishment, debased by ignorance, poverty and vice, could not be restrained to rational action. But the world will recover from the panic of this first catastrophe. Science is progressive, and talents and enterprize on the alert. Resort may be had to the people of the country, a more governable power from their principles and subordination; and rank, and birth, and tinsel-aristocracy will finally shrink into insignificance, even there. This however we have no right to meddle with. It suffices for us, if the moral and physical condition of our own citizens qualifies them to select the able and good for the direction of their government, with a recurrence of elections at such short periods as will enable them to displace an unfaithful servant before the mischief he meditates may be irremediable.

I have thus stated my opinion on a point on which we differ, not with a view to controversy, for we are both too old to change opinions which are the result of a long life of inquiry and reflection; but on the suggestion of a former letter of yours, that we ought not to die before we have explained ourselves to each other. We acted in perfect harmony thro' a long and perilous contest for our liberty and independence. A constitution has been acquired which tho neither of us think perfect, yet both consider as competent to render our fellow-citizens the happiest and the securest on whom the sun has ever shone. If we do not think exactly alike as to it's imperfections, it matters little to our country which, after devoting to it long lives of disinterested labor, we have delivered over to our successors in life, who will be able to take care of it, and of themselves.

*Adams* (Koch and Peden, *Adams*, pp. 169–70.)

We are now explicitly agreed, in one important point, vizt. That "there is a natural Aristocracy among men; the grounds of which are Virtue and Talents."

You very justly indulge a little merriment upon this solemn subject of Aristocracy. I often laugh at it too, for there is nothing in this laughable world more ridiculous than the management of it by almost all the nations of the Earth. But while We smile, Mankind have reason to say to Us, as the froggs said to the Boys, What is Sport to you is Wounds and death to Us. When I consider the weakness, the folly, the Pride, the Vanity, the Selfishness, the Artifice, the low craft and meaning cunning, the want of Principle, the Avarice the unbounded Ambition, the unfeeling Cruelty of a majority of those (in all Nations) who are allowed an aristocratical influence; and on the other hand, the Stupidity with which the more numerous multitude, not only become their Dupes, but even love to be Taken in by their Tricks: I feel a stronger disposition to weep at their destiny, than to laugh at their Folly.

But tho' We have agreed in one point, in Words, it is not yet certain that We are perfectly agreed in Sense. Fashion has introduced an indeterminate Use of the Word "Talents." Education, Wealth, Strength, Beauty, Stature, Birth, Marriage, graceful Attitudes and Motions, Gait, Air, Complexion, Physiognomy, are Talents, as well as Genius and Science and learning. Any one of these Talents, that in fact commands or influences two Votes in Society, gives to the Man who possesses it, the Character of an Aristocrat in my Sense of the Word.

Pick up, the first 100 men you meet, and make a Republick. Every Man will have an equal Vote. But when deliberations and discussions are opened it will be found that 25, by their Talents, Virtues being equal, will be able to carry 50 votes. Every one of these 25, is an Aristocrat, in my Sense of the Word; whether he obtains his one Vote in Addition to his own, by his Birth Fortune, Figure, Eloquence, Science, learning, Craft Cunning, or even his Character for good fellowship and a bon vivant.

What gave Sir William Wallace his amazing Aristocratical Superiority? His Strength. What gave Mrs. Clark, her Aristocratical Influence to create Generals Admirals and Bishops? her Beauty. What gave Pompadour and Du Barry the Power of making Cardinals and Popes? their beauty. You have seen the Palaces of Pompadour and Du Barry: and I have lived for years in the Hotel de Velentinois, with Franklin who had as many Virtues as any of them. In the investigation of the meaning of the Word "Talents" I could write 630 Pages, as pertinent as John Taylors of Hazelwood. . . .

Your distinction between natural and artificial Aristocracy does not appear to me well founded. Birth and Wealth are conferred on some Men, as imperiously by Nature, as Genius, Strength or Beauty. The Heir is honours and Riches, and power has often no more merit in procuring these Advantages, than he has in obtaining an handsome face or an elegant figure. When Aristocracies, are established by human Laws and honour Wealth and Power are made hereditary by municipal Laws and political Institutions, then I acknowledge artificial Aristocracy to commence: but this never commences, till Corruption in Elections becomes dominant and uncontroulable. But this artificial Aristocracy can never last. The everlasting Envys, Jealousies, Rivalries and quarrells among them, their cruel rapacities upon the poor ignorant People their followers, compell these to sett up Caesar, a Demagogue to be a Monarch and Master, pour mettre chacun a sa place. Here you have the origin of all artificial Aristocracy, which is the origin of all Monarchy. And both artificial Aristocracy, and Monarchy, and civil, military, political and hierarchical Despotism, have all grown out of the natural Aristocracy of "Virtues and Talents." We, to be sure, are far remote from this. Many hundred years must roll away before We shall be corrupted. Our pure, virtuous, public spirited federative Republic will last for ever, govern the Globe and introduce the perfection of Man, his perfectability being already proved by Price Priestley, Condorcet Rousseau Diderot and Godwin. . . .

Your distinction between the aristoi and pseudo aristoi, will not help the matter. I would trust one as soon as the other with unlimited Power. The Law wisely refuses an Oath as a witness in his own cause to the Saint as well as to the Sinner.

No Romance would be more amusing, than the History of your Virginian and our new England Aristocratical Families. Yet even in Rhode Island, where there has been no Clergy, no Church, and I had almost said, no State, and some People say no religion, there has been a constant respect for certain old Families. 57 or 58 years ago, in company with Col. Counsellor, Judge, John Chandler, whom I have quoted before, a Newspaper was brought in. The old Sage asked me to look for the News from Rhode Island and see how the Elections had gone there. I read the List of Wantons, Watsons, Greens, Whipples, Malbones etc. 'I expected as much' said the aged Gentleman, 'for I have always been of Opinion, that in the most popular Governments, the Elections will generally go in favour of the most ancient families.' To this day when any of these Tribes and We may Add Ellerys, Channings Champlins etc are pleased to fall in with the popular current, they are sure to carry all before them.

You suppose a difference of Opinion between You and me, on the Subject of Aristocracy. I can find none. I dislike and detest hereditary honours, Offices Emoluments established by Law. So do you. I am for ex[c]luding legal hereditary distinctions from the U.S. as long as possible. So are you. I only say that Mankind have not yet discovered any remedy against irresistable Corruption in Elections to Offices of great Power and Profit, but making them hereditary.

# VI

# FAREWELL

THE CORRESPONDENCE WAS A "CORDIAL" THAT WARMED THE HEARTS OF THE two old statesmen, and therefore they did not let it languish. Indeed, it lasted until just three months before the day they died. Jefferson's last letter to Adams introduced his grandson. (Lester J. Cappon, ed., *The Adams-Jefferson Letters*, 2 vols. [Chapel Hill: Univ. of North Carolina Press, 1959], II, 614.)]

LIKE OTHER young people, he wishes to be able, in the winter night of old age to recount to those around him what he has heard and learnt of the Heroic age preceding his birth, and which of the Argonauts particularly he was in time to have seen. It was the lot of our early years to witness nothing but the dull monotony of colonial subservience, and of our riper ones to breast the labors and perils of working out of it. Theirs are the Halcyon calms succeeding the storm which our Argosy had so stoutly weathered. Gratify his ambition then by receiving his best bow. . . .

[And Adams' last letter to his friend had the unmistakable Adams tone, magical in part because of its bright petulance, its surprises. (Cappon, *Adams-Jefferson Letters*, II, 614.)]

. . .WE NEW Englanders are but Pygmies by the side of Mr. Randolph. I was very much gratified with Mr. Randolph, and his conversation. Your letter is one of the most beautiful and delightful I have ever received.

Public affairs go on pretty much as usual: perpetual chicanery and rather more personal abuse than there used to be. Messrs. Randolph and McDuffie [both Southerners, and both opponents in Congress of President John Quincy Adams' administration] have out-Heroded Herod. Mr. McDuffie seems to be swallowed up in chivalry. Such institutions ought not to be suffered in a republican Government. Our American

Chivalry is the worst in the World. It has no Laws, no bounds, no definitions; it seems to be all a Caprice. My love to all your family, and best wishes for your health.

[These last two letters are strangely symbolic of the characters of these great men. Jefferson recalled the service in the cause of liberty wherein he honestly thought Adams had made his great contribution to his country and to posterity. It was the same cause which he himself revered above all others, terming it "the holy cause of liberty." And alive to the perspective of the young man he was sheltering, he suggested the passage of generations, their different tasks in winning and extending human freedoms. Adams loved the thought, too (that was why he found the letter "beautiful and delightful"), just as he adored the classical sound of a "Heroic age" in which he was an "Argonaut." But he preferred to comment on what his observant old eyes had not missed—the fact that the Virginians were tall; Virginia versus New England, the North and the South; the tragi-comedy of politics, with its unquenchable abuses, rivalry, posturing; even the fraud and the paradox of democracy suggested by "American chivalry is the worst in the world, all a Caprice." Characteristic, too, is that his very last words were love and wishes for his old friend's health.

As the fiftieth anniversary of the Declaration of Independence approached, these two great men, who had been foremost in its preparation and composition, still survived: ninety-one year old John Adams, in his quiet home in Quincy; and eighty-three year old Thomas Jefferson, on his mountaintop in Charlottesville. The two aged statesmen had both been asked to participate in the half-century celebrations in honor of Independence, but each was too feeble and ill to encourage such plans. John Adams gave the local committee a message: "Independence forever!" When he was asked to add something to that sentiment, he was adamant. "Not one word more," he stated.

Fortunately for us, Adams wrote several letters reflecting on the day. In one letter, he wrote: "A memorable epoch in the annals of the human race; destined in future history to form the brightest or the blackest page, according to the use or the abuse of those political institutions by which they shall in time to come be shaped by the *human mind*." He also wrote in another letter. (C. F. Adams, *Works*, X, 417–18.)]

. . .AN EVENT sanctioned by fifty years of experience, and it will become memorable by its increasing age, in proportion as its success shall demonstrate the blessings it imparts to our beloved country, and the maturity it may attain in the progress of time.

Not these United States alone, but a mighty continent, the last discovered, but the largest quarter of the globe, is destined to date the period of its birth and emancipation from the 4th of July 1776.

Visions of future bliss in prospect, for the better condition of the human race, resulting from this unparalleled event, might be indulged, but sufficient unto the day be the glory thereof. . . .

[Two weeks later Thomas Jefferson wrote a letter, now deservedly famous, in which he declined the invitation and reviewed the meaning of a document "pregnant with our own and the fate of the world." He too called attention to the consolatory fact that after half a century of experience his fellow-citizens continued to approve the choice which the Declaration announced. (Koch and Peden, *Jefferson*, 729–30.)]

MAY IT be to the world, what I believe it will be (to some parts sooner, to others later, but finally to all), the signal of arousing men to burst the chains under which monkish ignorance and superstition had persuaded them to bind themselves, and to assume the blessings and security of self-government. That form which we have substituted, restores the free right to the unbounded exercise of reason and freedom of opinion. All eyes are opened, or opening, to the rights of man. The general spread of the light of science has already laid open to every view the palpable truth, that the mass of mankind has not been born with saddles on their backs, nor a favored few booted and spurred, ready to ride them legitimately, by the grace of God. These are grounds of hope for others. For ourselves, let the annual return of this day forever refresh our recollections of these rights, and an undiminished devotion to them.

# FOR FURTHER READING

The best source for the joint correspondence of Adams and Jefferson is Lester Cappon, ed., *The Adams-Jefferson Letters*, 2 vols. (Chapel Hill: Univ. of North Carolina Press, 1959). The course of the brilliant correspondence reproduced here opens with the earliest letters they exchanged during the period of the Confederation at home and when they served abroad. The second volume is devoted entirely to letters from 1812–26, when, in retirement from public service, the two elder philosopher-statesmen reflected on the meaning of life, the nature of the universe, and the lessons of political history.

At present, two great editorial projects are in progress which aim to present complete collections of the work of these men. The first is Julian Boyd, ed., *The Papers of Thomas Jefferson* (Princeton, N.J.: Princeton Univ. Press, 1961) of which sixteen volumes have appeared out of a scheduled fifty-volume set. These volumes provide a definitive and complete record of the writings of Jefferson and the correspondence he received, and they are re-enforced by superb editorial notes and essays of invaluable aid to the student of Jefferson and the period. Volume XVI closes with July 1790. Of the second project, Lyman Butterfield, ed., *Adams Family Papers*, the first publication was *The Diary and Autobiography of John Adams*, 4 vols. (Cambridge, Mass.: Belknap Press of Harvard, 1961). This edition was never presented before in consecutive and definitive text, and it furnishes an intimate and remarkable record of John Adams' thoughts, values, emotions, and acts. The next sequence of volumes in preparation by Mr. Butterfield will be the Adams Family Correspondence.

Older collected editions do not live up to these standards. But for John Adams, see C. F. Adams, ed., *The Works of John Adams*, 10 vols. (Boston: Charles Little and James Brown, 1851) and for Thomas Jefferson, P. L. Ford, ed., *The Writings of Thomas Jefferson*, 10 vols. (New York: Putnam, 1893).

Convenient one-volume selections of the writings of Thomas Jefferson are Adrienne Koch and William Peden, *The Life and Selected Writings of Thomas Jefferson* (New York: Random House, Inc., Modern Library, 1944) and Bernard Mayo, *Jefferson Himself* (Boston: Houghton, 1942). Similarly, for one-volume selections of John Adams' writings see Adrienne Koch and William Peden, *Selected Writings of John and John Quincy Adams* (New York: Knopf, 1946) and George A. Peek, Jr., *The Political Writings of John Adams* (New York: Liberal Arts, 1954).

The best comprehensive biography of Thomas Jefferson is Dumas Malone's multi-volume study, *Jefferson and His Time*, three volumes of which have been published: *Jefferson the Virginian* (Boston: Little, 1948), *Jefferson and the Rights of Man* (1951), *Jefferson and the Ordeal of Liberty* (1962). Two more volumes are in preparation to complete the set. For a one-volume biography there is nothing which satisfies the several criteria of scholarship and analysis of ideas and readability. However, of the many one-volume biographies which have appeared in the twentieth century, the one which is based on a more extensive use of Jefferson's correspondence than any other and is generally informative is Gilbert Chinard's *Thomas Jefferson: Apostle of Americanism* (Boston: Little, 1939).

The most recent biography of Adams is Page Smith's two-volume study, *John Adams* (New York: Doubleday, 1962). Again, Gilbert Chinard's *Honest John Adams* (Boston: Little, 1933) must be cited as the one-volume biography in the twentieth-century.

For interpretations of various aspects of Jefferson's mind, one should consult the volume of essays assembled by Francis Coleman Rosenberger, ed., *Jefferson Reader* (New York: Dutton, 1953). For more intensive analysis, one may consult Adrienne Koch, *The Philosophy of Thomas Jefferson* (New York: Columbia Univ. Press, 1943), which concentrates on Jefferson's philosophical and moral reflections and Adrienne Koch, *Jefferson and Madison* (New York: Knopf, 1950), which studies his developing political thought in the context of his fifty-year collaboration with his friend, James Madison. A valuable study of one phase of Adams' intellectual interests is found in Zoltan Haraszti, *John Adams and the Prophets of Progress* (Cambridge: Harvard Univ. Press, 1952), which deals with Adams' marginal comments provoked by the works of eighteenth-century English and French political writers.